LIGHT FROM ANCIENT LETTERS

LIGHT FROM
ANCIENT LETTERS
PRIVATE CORRESPONDENCE IN THE
NON-LITERARY PAPYRI OF OXYRHYN-
CHUS OF THE FIRST FOUR CENTURIES,
AND ITS BEARING ON NEW TESTA-
MENT LANGUAGE AND THOUGHT

By HENRY G. MEECHAM, B.A.
(Lond.), M.A., B.D. (Manch.), *former
Wellington Scholar in the University of Manchester*

Wipf & Stock
PUBLISHERS
Eugene, Oregon

First published in 1923

Wipf and Stock Publishers
199 West 8th Avenue, Suite 3
Eugene, Oregon 97401

Light from Ancient Letters
Private correspondence in the non-literary papyri of Oxyrhynchus of the first four
centuries and its bearing on New Testament language and thought
By Meecham, Henry G.
ISBN: 1-59244-473-3
Publication date 1/15/2004
Previously published by George Allen & Unwin, 1923

TO

G. L. M.

PREFACE

THE following pages form the record of an attempt
to investigate one small corner of the wide field
of Hellenistic Greek, and to set forth therefrom
any data of significance for the literature of the New
Testament. Two names stand out pre-eminently.
The pioneer work of Dr. G. ADOLF DEISSMANN
(happily still with us) has given stimulus and
direction to all subsequent research. The writer
would pay special homage to the honoured memory
of the Rev. Dr. JAMES HOPE MOULTON, under
whose incomparable and genial guidance he was
first led to take interest in the linguistic relationships of the New Testament. That interest has
since been quickened by membership of the Hellenistic Seminar of Manchester University. The
writer's cordial thanks are due also to the Rev.
Dr. H. McLACHLAN for much kindly interest and
fruitful counsel. The essay herein presented is
offered as a humble contribution to a subject no
less fascinating than it is vital. Constant resort

to authorities has been made, as the footnotes will indicate.

Where citations are made from the papyri and New Testament, etc., the words in question have usually been quoted in the inflexional ending with which they appear in their original textual setting.

H. G. M.

Swinton, Manchester,
   November 1922.

CONTENTS

TABLE OF ABBREVIATIONS

O.T.   Old Testament.
N.T.   New Testament.
O.P.   Oxyrhynchus Papyri.
LXX.   Septuagint.
Art.   Article.
O.P.2.   Oxyrhynchus Papyri, No. 2.
G.H.   Grenfell & Hunt.
H.G.   Hellenistic Greek.
R.V.   Revised Version.
A.V.   Authorised Version.
M.Gr.   Modern Greek.
W.H.   N.T. in the original Greek (Westcott & Hort).
E.G.T.   Expositor's Greek Testament.
E.P.G.   Epistulæ Privatæ Græcæ (Witkowski), 2nd
              Edit.
M.M.   Vocabulary (Moulton and Milligan).
J.T.S.   Journal of Theological Studies.
M.T.   Moods and Tenses, etc. (Goodwin), 3rd Edit.
1/A.D.   First century of the Christian era.
1/2/A.D.   Between first and second centuries.
Select.   Selections from the Greek Papyri (Milligan).
Subj.   Subjunctive.
Indic.   Indicative.
Proleg.   Grammar of N.T. Greek, Vol. I. Prolegomena
              (Moulton), 3rd Edit.
N.T.D.   N.T. Documents (Milligan).
Eph.   Ephesians (and similarly with the names of
              books of Scripture).
H.D.B.   Dictionary of the Bible (ed. Hastings).

B.S.	Bible Studies (Deissmann), 2nd Edit.
L.A.E.	Light from the Ancient East (Deissmann), 2nd Edit.
κ.τ.λ.	καὶ τὰ λοιπά.
O.G.I.S.	Orientis Græci Inscriptiones Selectæ (ed. Dittenberger).
Archiv.	Archiv für Papyrusforschung (ed. Wilcken).
B.G.U.	Ægyptische Urkunden aus den Koeniglichen Museen zu Berlin.
Cent.B.	Century Bible.
R.V.m.	Margin of the R.V.
Encyc. Bib.	Encyclopedia Biblica.
l.	read.
cf.	compare.
p., pp.	page, pages.
f., ff.	and following verse(s), chapter(s), page(s), line(s).

N.B.—In the linguistic portions of this essay, the references are inserted in the body of the text in order to avoid too frequent reference to footnotes and so to facilitate reading.

In the enumeration, the first number relates to the papyrus under review, and following numbers to the lines in question, e.g. O.P. 292, 7 = O.P. No. 292, line 7.

LIGHT FROM ANCIENT LETTERS

INTRODUCTION

THE VALUE OF THE NON-LITERARY PAPYRI

GREEK was the language of the Hellenes, and reflects the high degree of cultural life which that people attained in the ancient world. In origin it belongs to the Aryan family. It is therefore cognate with the Germanic (itself a branch of the Aryan parent language) from which our own mother-tongue is derived. Hence the language in which the N.T. was originally written has a certain philological kinship, however far removed, with English. This fact is not without significance for the comprehension of the Christian message by the Western world. In reading the N.T. in the original, one is not led to remark that absence of linguistic affinity which soon makes itself apparent to the student of the O.T. The latter is essentially Semitic, and is to that extent foreign to Indo-European mentality.

An outstanding feature of ancient Greece was the remarkable dialectic diversity that sheltered within its narrow borders. The city-states, cut off from social intercourse by the mountainous character of the country, vied with each other in maintaining their individuality. Political autonomy was reflected in the varieties of dialect that obtained. The geographical contiguity of the separate Greek communities served to emphasise their differences of speech. Of these, Attic, the language of the Athenians, was confessedly *primus inter pares*, and when we speak of classical Greek it is mainly, though not exclusively, the Attic form that is in mind. In wealth of inflexion, range of vocabulary and richness of tense-system, in its qualities of subtlety and grace, Attic Greek has never been surpassed. It was an incomparable vehicle for the lucid expression of delicate thought and feeling.

Post-classical Greek [1] is marked more and more by deviations from the rigorous Attic standard mainly in vocabulary, but also in grammar. Valiant attempts were made to preserve a pure Attic strain. It was the ambition of every literary aspirant to write in the archaic yet canonical language of the past. This Atticistic revival reached its climax in the second century A.D. Despite all such efforts, however, the language became freely coloured with elements of different dialectic origin as well as with those drawn directly from the vernacular. To this artificial literary language which remained, notwithstanding admixture, pre-eminently Attic in groundwork, the term " literary Koinē " (καθαραεύουσα) has been applied in contrast with the " oral Koinē " (ὁμιλουμένη) or spoken dialect of daily life. The one savoured of

[1] Aristotle (d. 322 B.C.) may be taken as marking the approximate end of the classical period.

the study, the other of the street. In this book the term κοινή is used to cover both types, that is, the literary and the vernacular, which are again severally distinguished, where necessary, by the terms "literary Koinē" and "oral Koinē" respectively.

Life spells movement. Language, which is the expression of life, is therefore always in flux. Outward change in the life of a nation leads to enlargement of its experience and development of its thought, and these in turn are mirrored in its speech. The course of Greek history provides a clear example of the process. Philip of Macedon (382–336 B.C.) had brought about by force of arms the political unification of Greece, and the free communication thus established between the various states tended to wear down dialectic peculiarities. The conquests of Alexander the Great (356–323 B.C.) gave a great impetus to the circulation of a common Greek. The culture of the Greeks spread to Egypt and Asia Minor. In camp and tent, men from all localities, Spartan, Ionian and Bœotian, were herded together, with the inevitable result that dialectic differences increasingly disappeared. Within a few generations varieties of dialect fused into a common colloquial language. The vernacular Attic developed naturally into a vernacular κοινή. Thus by this pooling process a kind of average Greek was evolved. The need of a common medium of intercourse for commercial purposes in the lands thus opened out hastened the development. Peculiarities that were merely local tended to drop out, leaving a common residuum. The resultant lan-

guage was thus composite. Orthographically, it
subscribed to the standard literary model, Attic ;
orally, it still preserved traces of its original
dialectic diversity. That there was practically no
dialectic variation, except in pronunciation, in the
far-spread Hellenistic Greek (this term is used as
almost synonymous with the term κοινή) is a fact
of striking import to the student of the science
of language. MOULTON [1] says : " On the question of the contribution of the old dialects to the
κοινή, research seems progressively emphasising the
preponderance of Attic." It seems clear that
the vernacular Attic was the common base of the
κοινή. According to Dr. A. T. ROBERTSON [2] the
period of the κοινή extended from 300 B.C. to
A.D. 330.

The transition from Hellenistic to Modern
Greek in accordance with the principle of con-
tinuous development stated above does not concern us here, save to remark that all the essential
elements of Modern Greek have been transmitted
through the vernacular κοινή.[3] Enough has perhaps been said to show the historical genesis of
Hellenistic Greek and its place in the line of
descent. It remains now briefly to stress two
further points. First, the essential kinship of the
N.T. writings with the spoken κοινή of the
Hellenistic world. The former cannot be adequately paralleled from the literary κοινή of the
period as seen in the writings of Polybius and
Josephus. There are, it is true, as Dr. H. A. A.

[1] *Prolegomena*, p. 41, note.
[2] *A Grammar of the Greek N.T.*, p. 43 (3rd Edit.).
[3] So MOULTON, *op. cit.*, p. 32 ; see examples on pp. 81–83
(*infra*).

KENNEDY [1] has shown, some slight vocabular
affinities of the N.T. with Philo, Strabo and other
penmen of the literary κοινή. But, in the main,
the body of the N.T. Scriptures is composed in
what the papyri and inscriptions are plainly
revealing was the common Greek of the Empire.
The isolation of N.T. language conferred upon
it by such terms as " Biblical," " Judaic," etc.,
finds no support in the new discoveries. The
descriptive adjective that can most fittingly be
prefixed to the Greek of the N.T. is " common."
To quote from Dr. A. T. ROBERTSON [2] again :
" The N.T. Greek is now seen to be not an abnormal
excrescence, but a natural development in the
Greek language ; to be, in fact, a not unworthy
part of the great stream of the mighty tongue.
It was not outside of the world-language, but in
the very heart of it, and influenced considerably
the future of the Greek tongue." Only in a limited
sense is it now legitimate to use the term " N.T.
Greek," that is, as the language of a collection
of books which may lay just claim to uniqueness
on other than linguistic grounds. That there are
literary elements, Hebraistic phrases, and Latin-
isms in the N.T. is obvious, but that fact in no
way invalidates its kinship with the vernacular
of its day. N.T. Greek is not a separate variety
of the Greek tongue. The witness of the papyri on
this vital point is invaluable. Supposed Semitisms
in the N.T. hitherto explained as due to unconscious reminiscences of Septuagint terminology,
or to the habit of thinking in Aramaic and writing
in Greek, or again (where Aramaic sources may

[1] *Sources of N.T. Greek*, p. 50 f   [2] *Grammar*, p. 30.

be posited) to over-literal translation, are now
copiously illustrated from Egyptian papyri. (The
point whether these papyri-usages themselves
may be due to Jewish influence in Egypt falls to
be discussed in Chapter VII, p. 162.) Hebraistic
strata are to be found in the N.T., but they are
not so extensive as was formerly supposed.

The other point which calls for mention is the
wide diffusion of the κοινή. Greek letters and
civilisation spread over a very wide area. The
inscriptions show that the Greek language had
reached Italy, Egypt, Asia Minor and the islands
of the sea. MOULTON [1] points out " that in the
first centuries of our era Greek covered a far
larger proportion of the civilised world than even
English does to-day." It had become practically
coextensive with Western civilisation. Hence its
peculiar fitness to be the vehicle of a world-faith.
" When the fulness of the time came " a universal
language was Providentially raised to convey a
universal message to a world-empire cemented by
a common rule. So we find that Paul writing his
encyclical to Rome, and Marcus Aurelius, the
Roman Emperor, composing his famous " Medi-
tations," both employ Greek. Coupled with this
is the fact that Hellenistic Greek is simpler and
far less subtle than its classical predecessor. It
lends itself easily to literal translation, and so can
be rendered into other languages with the minimum
of loss. In the words of Dr. MOFFATT,[2] " it is an
eminently translatable language, and the evidence
of papyrology shows that it was more flexible

[1] *Prolegomena*, p. 5.
[2] *The N.T.: A New Translation*, Preface, p. v (5th Edit.).

than once was imagined." In view of such features we hold that Hellenistic Greek merits study and research not as the offspring (degenerate, as some think) of the classical tongue, but as possessing intrinsic dignity and value.

Leaving out of reckoning the literary κοινή of Polybius and Josephus on the one hand and Modern Greek on the other, both of which are of value in the study of N.T. language, it is clear that the greatest worth attaches to the non-literary memorials, especially the papyri, of Hellenistic Greek. Fortunately, these form by far the major part of the relics. Literary production as such rarely escapes some degree of artificiality and affectation since, admittedly, it is intended for publicity. The *littérateur* writes with an audience in view. Reputation is more or less at stake. Hence he will exercise care to write correctly and in a style that will not offend the accepted canons of literary taste. Self-consciousness is therefore almost inevitable in his work, and the degree of his artistic instinct will be the measure of his tendency as an author to mere literary artifice and restraint. On the contrary, non-literary writings, just because they are not usually intended for public or permanent use, are to a high degree self-revealing, naïve and unconsciously suggestive. Broadly speaking, the literary relics reflect the thought and speech of the educated upper classes, the non-literary that of the lower classes. In private letters especially the varied life of the common people stands self-portrayed. DEISSMANN,[1] quoting VON WILAMOWITZ-

[1] *Bible Studies*, p. 11, note.

Moellendorff, says : " Such letters as are actually written with a view to publication are essentially different in character from private correspondence." Two features of the N.T. writings must here be recalled. In the first place, primitive Christianity was pre-eminently a movement among the masses.[1] Fishermen, artisans and slaves found ample room in its ranks. It is true that wealth and social prestige were not unrepresented among the followers of Jesus, e.g. Nicodemus (John iii. 1), Joseph of Arimathæa (Matt. xxvii. 57), etc., and that is a factor which must not be left out of account. But in the main, " not many mighty, not many noble are called " (1 Cor. i. 26). It is reasonable, therefore, to expect in the N.T. some indication of that stratum of lower middle-class life and thought to which the adherents of early Christianity chiefly belonged. Deissmann [2] sums up : " The chief and most general value of the non-literary written memorials of the Roman Empire, I think, is this : they help us to correct the picture of the ancient world which we have formed by viewing it, hitherto, exclusively from above." Only by writing in the popular language could the N.T. authors hope to reach the common people. Secondly, the sacred writers had no knowledge that their work would rank as literature. For one thing, they shared the current view of the early return of the Lord and the speedy consummation of the existing world-order.[3] For another, the occasion of many of the N.T. books

---

[1] Cf. Mark xii. 37 ; 1 Cor. vii. 20–24 ; Philemon.
[2] *Light from the Ancient East,* p. 8.
[3] Cf. 1 Thess. iv. 15 ; Matt. x. 23.

(especially is this true of the Epistles) was some particular need or exigency which, since the Second Advent was regarded as imminent, could not in the nature of things last very long. The N.T. books were chiefly intended for the early Christian communities or addressed to particular individuals, e.g. the Epistle to Philemon. Their origin and purpose determined largely their non-literary character. As MOULTON [1] says : " They wrote for immediate needs, in a world they thought near to its end, and they had neither time nor taste for literary canons."

It is but natural, therefore, to find in the non-literary papyri our first and most fruitful source for the fuller understanding of N.T. language and thought, notwithstanding Dr. D. S. MARGOLIOUTH's stricture quoted by Dr. ROBERTSON [2] that " not one per cent. of those which are deciphered and edited with so much care tell us anything worth knowing." A word must suffice on their obvious value for palæography. Speaking of the papyrus period, Sir F. G. KENYON [3] says : " Its real importance lies in the fact that it is the period to which the autographs of the N.T. belong, and that by indirect means we can learn something as to the appearance of these autographs and of the conditions under which the Christian Scriptures circulated during the first three centuries of their existence." The main importance of the non-literary papyri for N.T. study is twofold, linguistic

[1] Art. on *The Language of the N.T.* (PEAKE's *Comm. on Bible*, p. 591).

[2] *Grammar,* p. x.

[3] *Handbook to the Textual Criticism of the N.T.*, pp. 18–19.

and historical. Linguistically, they are proving to be of greater value than the inscriptions. The latter incline to be cold, formal and lifeless ; the former are invariably fresh, natural and un-adorned. DEISSMANN [1] writes : " The inscriptions are often cold and dead things like the marble on which they are carved. The papyrus leaf is alive ; one sees autographs, individual peculiarities of penmanship—in a word, men ; manifold glimpses are given into inmost nooks and crannies of per-sonal life for which history has no eyes and historians have no glasses." The evidence of the linguistic data so profusely poured forth by the non-literary documents in general (evidence which we hope to show is confirmed by our present particularised enquiry) is conclusive for the view that in vocabulary and grammar the writers of the N.T. used the colloquial late Greek of their day, which was syntactically much simpler than the classical language. (The necessary modifica-tion of this statement which is called for by the undoubted occurrence of Semitisms in the N.T. falls to be discussed in Chapter VII (see p. 158 f.)). It is further to be observed that the very illiteracy of many papyri, with their harsh concords and flagrant misspellings, is of great significance as showing the grammatical tendency of the lan-guage. Violation of and deviation from literary canons may often prove highly instructive in tracing the historical growth of a language.

The historical significance of the papyri lies in the light they throw upon the environment of nascent Christianity, and in those instances where

[1] *Encyc. Bib.*, col. 3558.

they bear upon the historical trustworthiness of the N.T. record. Of the latter point a good example appears in the discovery of census-returns (ἀπογραφαί) which verify Luke's historical accuracy in Luke ii. 1–2, and illustrate the method of enumeration there specified.[1] With regard to the more general revivification of early Christian times thus effected, it is no serious defect that all the papyri (with the exception of the find at Herculaneum in 1752) come from the sands of Egypt. For the student of the LXX that fact means a positive gain, since it was in Ptolemaic Egypt that the Greek O.T. was produced, and the degree of its Egyptianisation is by no means a negligible factor. Indeed, as DEISSMANN[2] points out, the distinctively Egyptian character of the LXX can only be made plain by its comparison with the literary relics of contemporary Egypt. But for the purpose of N.T. research also, the Egyptian origin of the papyri is far from being disadvantageous. Important cities like Alexandria formed strategic centres of early Christian culture. Greek-speaking Jews settled in large numbers on the banks of the Nile and in that cosmopolitan environment Christianity took deep root. The papyri of Upper Egypt, mirroring as they do the many-sided life of the people, cannot fail to convey vivid impressions of the background against which early Greek Christianity should be viewed.[3] More-

[1] Cf. P. Brit. Mus. 904, and G. MILLIGAN's *Selections*, etc., p. xxviii, 44–45.

[2] *Bible Studies*, p. 70.

[3] The geographical limitations of the papyri are amply compensated for by their immense variety in contents.

over, so far as concerns language, the inscriptions corroborate to a large extent the witness of the papyri, thus showing that there was no well-marked dialectic difference between the Greek of Egypt and that of Asia Minor.[1] Further, the chronological extent of the papyri evidence should be noted. MOULTON[2] dates the papyri from 311 B.C. to the seventh century A.D. Thus they cover roughly a thousand years, and offer a valuable index to the history of Græco-Roman Egypt during that period. In character and contents immense diversity is found. Wills, leases, receipts, memoranda, contracts, decrees, petitions and private letters meet the eye in bewildering profusion. The last-named in particular are replete with human interest ; but the whole heterogeneous mass is valuable in its incidental allusions and the glimpses so ingenuously given into the social, domestic and business relationships of the people. The recurrence of fixed formulæ and stereotyped phrases makes for monotony ; but it is both relieved and redeemed by the suggestive allusions that now and again light up the picture. The spontaneity and entire absence of elaboration which mark these unschooled remains constitute both their charm and worth. Though fragmentary and detached, when pieced together they form a rich mosaic. The historic origin of a religion can best be understood through that type of literature in which its character and conditions are most faithfully depicted. It is not the least among the benefits brought by the Egyptian

[1] *Vide supra*, pp. 17–18.
[2] *Proleg.*, p. 27.

non-literary documents that they render this signal service to Christianity.[1]

A word as to the scope, method and aim of this book. The non-literary papyri have been chosen because, for reasons advanced above, they are of first-hand importance for the interpretation of N.T. language and thought. Private letters have been selected because the epistolary element is integral to the N.T. literature, and because, in LIGHTFOOT's classical words quoted by Professor G. MILLIGAN,[2] " if we could only recover letters that ordinary people wrote to each other without any thought of being literary, we should have the greatest possible help for the understanding of the language of the N.T. generally." That " greatest possible help " is now to hand in the artless letters unearthed in Egypt. To quote Professor MILLIGAN[3] again: " An Egyptian papyrus-letter and a N.T. epistle may be widely separated alike by the nationality and habitat of their writers and by their own inherent characters and aims, but both are written in substantially the same Greek." The enquiry has been delimited to Oxyrhynchus, partly because of the obvious necessity of a definitely localised source (since papyri collections have grown to such large proportions), and partly because it is that field which has so far proved the most prolific. It is to be noted, however, that Dr. EDOUARD NAVILLE[4] states that on the site of the old Thmuis he found

[1] *Vide infra*, Chapter VI.   [2] *Selections*, p. xx.
[3] *N.T. Documents*, p. 49.
[4] COBERN's *New Archæological Discoveries*, etc., p. xviii (2nd Edit.).

thousands of Greek papyri which, had they been sufficiently preserved, would have rivalled those of Oxyrhynchus in numbers and interest. The restriction of the documentary evidence to the first four centuries of the Christian era is due to the fact that that period is for our present purpose the most important. It is not, of course, to be regarded as exhaustive in the interpretation of Christian origins.

Within these severe limits the aim of the essay is to show (1) how far the writers of the N.T. are affected by the language of everyday life, that is, to strengthen or modify the claim made by modern N.T. scholarship that the language of the N.T. is mainly that of ordinary conversation rather than of literature. (2) What light is thrown by these letters on the epistolary forms of the N.T. (3) Any points of coincidence or contrast with the N.T. in thought or subject-matter. It is perhaps scarcely necessary to add that, in view of the limits of the thesis as here defined, none of its findings is claimed in any sense as final. Where inductions which these private letters seem to justify are made, they are wholly tentative and require to be confirmed or qualified by data drawn from a much wider area. No habit of mind is more unscientific than that of making generalisations on the basis of limited or isolated phenomena. Only that linguistic evidence which derives from far-extended sources, and which is, in the main, consistent with itself, ought to be presumed as conclusive. Even then it must always be subject to revision or rejection in the light of the new discoveries which time may bring.

It remains only to state that the text of the N.T. used throughout this study is that presented in SOUTER'S *Novum Testamentum Grœce.* The text of the LXX is that of the Cambridge edition edited by SWETE.

CHAPTER I

BRIEF HISTORICAL ACCOUNT OF THE OXYRHYNCHUS PAPYRI

THE history of the discovery of Greek papyri in Egypt may be said to begin with the year 1778, when some fifty papyrus documents were found at Gizeh. Of these only one has been preserved, and is now housed in the museum at Naples. A period of twenty years elapsed, and then occasional discoveries, mainly on the site of the ancient Memphis, were reported. Public interest in these first-fruits of excavation was not, however, fully awakened until 1877. In that year large numbers of papyri, greatly diversified in contents and chronology, and of a non-literary character, were discovered at Arsinoe in the Fayûm district, a region that has proved singularly prolific in papyri deposits. Then followed a find by Dr. W. M. FLINDERS PETRIE in the cemetery at Hawara, 1888–90. The papyri then unearthed contained valuable literary fragments and many ancient wills of the third century B.C.[1] The story of the Oxyrhynchus yield dates from 1897, when Pro-

[1] Professor G. MILLIGAN deals with the discovery and publication of papyri in the *Expositor*, March 1918.

fessor B. P. GRENFELL and Dr. A. S. HUNT, two
distinguished Oxford scholars who had begun work
in that area in 1894, laid bare a large and valuable
quantity of Greek papyri at Behnesa, the desolate
site of the ancient Oxyrhynchus. One of the chief
cities of Egypt, situate in the Fayûm valley, about
a hundred and twenty miles from the banks of
the Nile, Oxyrhynchus was the capital of a nome
or province. The name ("sharp-snouted") is a
Greek designation supposed to signify the species
of fish, probably a pike, the worship of which
formed a chief element in the local cultus.[1] After
the introduction of Christianity into Egypt, Oxyrhynchus flourished as an important monastic
centre. By the sixth century it had become one
of the leading Christian cities of Egypt. Its
evidential value for our knowledge of Egyptian
Christian thought and environment is therefore
apparent. It occasions no surprise that the
rubbish-dumps of Oxyrhynchus have proved a
fruitful field.

The first find of Drs. GRENFELL and HUNT was
soon perceived to be one of exceptional interest
and significance. Among many theological and
classical texts covering the first seven centuries
of the Christian era, an excerpt from a papyrus
book which purported to be a collection of Sayings
of Jesus excited immediate and widespread attention. These reputed Λογία ’Ιησοῦ (eight in number) were published in the same year, under the
title of *Sayings of our Lord*, by the Egypt Exploration Fund Society. A period of six years passed
before the explorers were able to return to the

[1] Cf. J. O. BEVAN'S *Egypt and the Egyptians*, p. 265.

Oxyrhynchite area, but in 1903 a further large addition to papyri stores was made from that source. Time was needed to bring out the linguistic and historical bearing of the miscellaneous mass of memoranda, wills, leases and letters, etc., which the spade upturned. But for the moment theological interest again predominated in that *New Sayings of Jesus and Fragment of a Lost Gospel* were brought to the light. The λέγει 'Ιησοῦς of these documents evoked a voluminous discussion which has raged round the question of the genuineness of the sayings. The crux lies there. "What value have they (the reputed sayings of Jesus), if any, for Christian faith and thought ? What determinative influence do they exercise over our spiritual and intellectual attitude towards Jesus ? The answer is largely dependent upon such solution as may be found concerning the authenticity or otherwise of these sayings. Are these genuine utterances of Jesus or not ? If they are, then they come to us with all the authority of the Great Teacher, despite the fact that they find no place within the limits of Holy Writ. Could it be proved that they were in actual fact the very words of Jesus, they would forthwith become canonical for us. But the fact is that proof here, as so often elsewhere, is not possible The most we can gain is strong intrinsic probability. Some are well attested and afford a very strong presumption that they go back to the primitive evangelic tradition." [1] The editors judged the two sets of Logia to be practically

[1] Art. by the present writer in the *Holborn Review* January 1916, p. 94.

contemporary, and dated them in the third century A.D.

Since 1904 excavations at Oxyrhynchus have proceeded without any serious intermission. The wealth of the quarry has become increasingly manifest. Year by year fresh volumes of Egypt Exploration Fund Reports have borne witness to the untiring labours of Drs. GRENFELL and HUNT in discovery, decipherment and interpretation. Fifteen volumes, comprising from the Oxyrhynchus field alone 1,828 papyri, have so far been issued. Apparently the mine is not yet worked out.[1]

As apposite to the general subject of the present study it may be of interest to note that Oxyrhynchus has yielded some important manuscripts of the N.T. Professor G. MILLIGAN [2] gives a list of Oxyrhynchan N.T. manuscripts, based upon the notation adopted by Professor C. R. GREGORY. It may be pointed out that some five or six of the MSS. are estimated to date from the third century, and are therefore presumably older than the two great N.T. uncials א (Codex Sinaiticus) and B (Codex Vaticanus) which derive from the fourth century.

[1] The O.P. series is likely to exceed thirty volumes. So Dr. GRENFELL in *John Ryland's Library Bulletin*, vol. vi. p. 149.

[2] *N.T.D.*, p. 248 f.

CHAPTER II

OXYRHYNCHAN PRIVATE CORRESPON-
DENCE—ITS EXTENT, CHARACTER
AND CLASSIFICATION

1. Extent.

THE following list indicates the papyri read and examined as the basis of this essay. It comprises all the private letters of the first four centuries found in vols. i–xv of the O.P. The point is not without significance for estimating the extent of the practice of letter-writing in early Christian times that out of a total of 1,828 papyri from Oxyrhynchus some 224 are of the nature of private correspondence (208 papyri from the first four centuries and 16 from a later period). The relatively large number of private letters in the chief papyri collections, together with the fact of their diversified contents (they are rich in human interest and are as many-sided as life itself) go to show that letter-writing in the ancient world was not confined to special occasions or restricted to important business, but that people wrote freely about the trivial happenings of daily life. The habit of letter-writing was apparently quite general among all sections of the community.

The antiquity of the practice is worth noting. Professor MILLIGAN [1] says : " The earliest mention of the art of writing in the *Iliad* (vi. 168 ff.) is in connection with a letter, and we actually possess an original Greek letter inscribed on a leaden tablet, which dates from the fourth century before Christ."

Vol.	I.	Nos.	110–124.
,,	II.	,,	291–300, 396–400.
,,	III.	,,	523–533, 582, 587, 589, 597–599, 602, 608, 642, 644.
,,	IV.	,,	742–747, 787, 789, 791, 805, 811–813, 819–822, 829, 839.
,,	V.	,,	None.
,,	VI.	,,	926–939, 963, 967.
,,	VII.	,,	1061–1070.
,,	VIII.	,,	1153–1162.
,,	IX.	,,	1213–1223.
,,	X.	,,	1291–1299, 1345–1349.
,,	XI.	,,	None.
,,	XII.	,,	1479–1495, 1579–1593.
,,	XIII.	,,	None.
,,	XIV.	,,	1663–1684, 1755–1777.
,,	XV.	,,	None.

Total number of letters examined, 208.

2. Character.

DEISSMANN [2] draws a fundamental distinction between a " letter " and an " epistle." Identical in form, they are yet quite dissimilar in essence.

[1] *N.T.D.*, pp. 85–6.
[2] *Bible Studies*, pp. 3–59.

A letter is a private communication between persons whom distance deters from personal colloquy. "The more faithfully it catches the tone of the private conversation, the more of a letter, that is, the better a letter, it is."[1] Its circle is strictly limited to the author and its recipient(s). To that extent a letter is a confidential missive. Not a word of it is for the public eye. Hence a "true letter" is intimate and personal, and its contents are rightly regarded by convention as sacred. Charged with his thought and feeling, it becomes in high degree a self-revelation of its author. It is the spontaneous outpouring of his soul. Anything in the nature of elaboration or artifice is utterly foreign to its purpose. A true letter is artless and non-literary, or rather "pre-literary," as Professor V. BARTLET[2] prefers to call it. It is "akin to a diary." We may add to these various characteristics the fact that letters, because they are a natural reflection of personal life with its many-sided experiences and interests, are often of the most varied contents. The letter, in short, has a distinctive aim, namely, the maintenance through writing of frank and intimate intercourse. This means that it can only be adequately interpreted in close relationship with its writer and reader(s) and their circumstances.

The epistle, on the other hand, is, *per se*, a literary document. Its aim is avowedly general. The wider its circulation, the more fully is its purpose met. Hence an epistle is usually restrained and

---

[1] *Op. cit.*, p. 3.
[2] Art. *Epistle* (*H.D.B.*, vol. i. p. 730).

impersonal. It casts little, if any, direct light upon the personality of its author. Written with an eye upon the public, it can hardly escape a certain literary flavour. And lastly, in the nature of the case, its contents will be found, as a rule, to be restricted to a definite theme rather than to subsist in a wealth of trivial, personal detail. DEISSMANN [1] sums up : " The one is a product of literary art, the other is a bit of life."

The distinction thus formulated by the great German pioneer is valid in the main. The criticism might be maintained that he scarcely allows sufficient room, by this sharp dichotomy, for the intermediate species, that is, books which suggest a fainter line of demarcation between " letter " and " epistle." But it is specially in the application of DEISSMANN's test to the N.T. epistles that caution needs to be exercised. Certainly his claim that *all* the Pauline writings are letters rather than epistles calls for qualification. " He (Paul) wrote letters, real letters, as did Aristotle and Cicero, as did the men and women of the Fayûm. They differ from the messages of the homely papyrus leaves from Egypt, not as letters, but only as the letters of Paul." [2] DEISSMANN goes on to apply the dictum to both Romans and Philemon alike.[3]   The question of the category into which the N.T. epistles may be placed falls to be discussed in Chapter V.[4] The present point

[1] Art. *Epistolary Literature* (*Encyc. Bib.*, col. 1324).

[2] *Bible Studies*, p. 44.

[3] Sir W. M. RAMSAY (*The Teaching of Paul, etc.*, p. 427 f.) subjects DEISSMANN's view to a searching criticism.

[4] See below, p. 101 f., 109 f.

is to claim that these papyrus letters are, by all
DEISSMANN's tests, rightly judged to be " true
letters." They bear upon their face the indelible
stamp of genuineness. We have included in our
selection strictly private letters only, for the
reason that here we find the writers taken, so to
speak, off their guard. Their words are unstudied,
fresh, human. In a real sense the letter is the man.
Petitionary letters to officials (which species was
probably antecedent to private correspondence),[1]
have been excluded as necessarily involving, in
some degree, the formal and unnatural. As Dr.
A. S. PEAKE [2] says : " Especially the familiar
unstudied letters, written with no thought that
any eye but that of the recipient would ever rest
upon them, but now scrutinised by scholars with
the keenest interest, touch us in their frank and
artless revelation of feeling, with that touch of
nature which makes the whole world kin."
Privacy, intimacy, depths of personal feeling,
frankness, artlessness and spontaneity—all these
essential qualities of a true letter are here in
abundance. There is not the slightest hint of
literary craftsmanship. The tone is colloquial
almost throughout. The varied contents hold up
the mirror to the inner life of both reader and
writer, to their interests and aspirations as to
their joys and fears. Numerous allusions, many
cryptic, are tantalising in their incompleteness,
making us feel again and again how much more
we could read between the lines of the letter if

[1] So BARTLET in *H.D.B.*, vol. i. p. 729.
[2] *The Bible, its Origin, Significance and Abiding Worth*,
p. 34.

we but knew more of its occasion and author. What could be better samples of true letters (to take three examples only) than No. 119 from Theon, junior, to his father, or No. 1162, a kindly letter of commendation, or that self-revealing message from a soldier-son which is found in No. 1481 ?

We conclude, therefore, that these letters are genuine instances of their kind. The fact that they have survived their brief day and are now accessible to a curious world in no way detracts from their original and distinctive character. For, as Dr. ROBERTSON [1] says, " a real letter that has become literature is different from an epistle written as literature."

3. Classification.

The question to be discussed in this section does not relate to the obvious twofold division—letters and epistles. As we have seen, all the papyri under review meet DEISSMANN'S cardinal test of a true letter. They are specimens of frank, intimate and personal communications, and are accordingly to be reckoned as real letters. It remains now further to subdivide this collection of letters and to determine into what categories they naturally and easily fall. In the main three bases of classification may be adopted. They are—

(a) *The standard of the writer's education.*

This is the criterion accepted by WITKOWSKI.[2] He classifies his selection of letters thus :—

[1] *Grammar*, p. 70.
[2] *Epistulæ Privatæ Græcæ*, pp. xiii–xv.

1. Epistulæ hominum eruditorum.
2.   ,,   ,,   modice eruditorum.
3.   ,,   ,,   non eruditorum.

The standard set up by WITKOWSKI is of value in that the degree of illiteracy in a letter is often of considerable linguistic significance as showing the grammatical direction of a language (see above, p. 24). Much may be learned from a writer's obvious errors. It has the further advantage that by grouping together the less educated writers it facilitates the enumeration and comparison of their grammatical blunders. But WITKOWSKI's test is open to the objection that it is sometimes very difficult to decide the degree of a writer's illiteracy. The division must at times be necessarily arbitrary.

(b) *The chronology of a letter.*

A collection of letters may be roughly classified according to the period or century to which they are assigned. This is the basis adopted by the editors of the O.P. The private correspondence is dated as deriving from the first, second or third century, etc. So far as general convenience is concerned, this method is probably the best. On the other hand, the difficulty (in some cases) of determining the chronology of a letter must be emphasised. The internal evidence, such as vocabulary, grammatical form as well as historical allusion, may be insufficient or conflicting, with the result that scholars widely disagree in their opinion concerning date. A good case in point is that of the Epistle of James, which some scholars, e.g. J. B. MAYOR,[1] G. B. STEVENS,[2] regard as pre-Pauline, and others, e.g. A. S. PEAKE,[3] assign to a date early in the second century. So in these papyri it frequently happens that an approximate date is all that can be established. The editors often date a letter thus, 1/2/A.D., that is, the letter lies on the border-line between the first and second centuries of the Christian era.

(c) The contents or substance of a letter.

This is the standard we adopt and for the following reasons :—

1. We stand on surer ground in making the contents of the letter the decisive factor in classification rather than the writer's literary attainments on the one hand or the probable date of his letter on the other. The subjective element in the critic has less room for licence. We may or may not be sure as to the writer's education or century, but what he writes about lies before us as clear and incontrovertible evidence.

2. As a rule, the main purport of a letter on papyrus is stated simply and briefly. It is the ornamentation—the numerous epistolary phrases and formal greetings—which occupies a relatively large space in the letter. The concise statement of the matter in hand makes it comparatively easy to detect in which of the following categories any letter should be placed.

3. Whilst it is true, as DEISSMANN [4] remarks,

---

[1] *The Epistle of St. James*, p. cxxi f.
[2] *The Theology of the N.T.*, pp. 249–52.
[3] *A Critical Introd. to the N.T.*, p. 87.
[4] *Bible Studies*, p. 4.

that the particular contents of a letter do not belong to the essence of it (that lies in the personal and confidential purpose which the letter is intended to serve), yet they do afford a means of classification which is both convenient and safe. The classification of the N.T. epistles as doctrinal, pastoral, private, etc., as against their chronological arrangement on the one hand or their literary excellence on the other, is analogous.

It is, however, to be noted that this method allows of only a rough classification. No hard-and-fast line can be drawn, since not infrequently a letter will contain business transactions mixed up with private and domestic news. A clear example of this intermixture of serious or semi-official details with personal and trivial matters is seen in O.P. 294, where the author, after writing about an impending lawsuit, suddenly breaks off into, " Let me hear about our bald friend, how his hair is growing again on the top! " For similar instances, cf. Nos. 298, 928.

Taking the substance of the letters as the basis of division, the O.P. relating to this study fall into the following classes :—

A. Personal and Domestic. (127.)

This class comprises by far the largest proportion of the private correspondence. A noteworthy feature is the number of family letters, that is, letters intended only for the members of the same domestic circle. These letters are full of fine and intimate allusions which now and again remind us of Paul's personal touches as felt especially in 2 Cor. and Phil. Detached letters, too, are found which, pieced together, help us to reconstruct in a measure some family history or domestic story. O.P. 275 is a case in point.[1]

113, 114, 115 (letter of condolence), 116, 118, 119 (from a schoolboy to his father), 120, 123, 293, 295 (strictly personal letter from a daughter to her mother), 298, 300, 396–400, 526, 528–529, 531 (from a father to his son, giving good advice, etc.), 532, 582, 587, 589, 598–599, 608, 644, 742–744, 789, 791, 805, 811–813, 819–822, 829, 839, 928–939, 963, 967, 1067, 1069, 1070, 1153–1155, 1159–1161, 1215–1218, 1222–1223, 1291–1299, 1345–1349, 1481, 1482, 1488–1495, 1581–1586, 1589–1593, 1666, 1670, 1676, 1678–1684, 1757, 1761, 1763–1764, 1766, 1768–1770, 1773–1774.

> N.B.—(a) 526, 528, 742, 1067, 1069, 1155, 1215–1216, 1482, 1670 are very illiterate.
>
> (b) 939, 1161, 1492–1495, 1592, 1774 strongly suggest Christian influence.

B. Semi-official. (14.)

122, 291, 294, 296, 297, 597, 602, 642, 1063, 1065, 1221, 1483, 1490, 1664.

> N.B.—122, 291, are letters written from superior officials to subordinates. The writer places his own name first, and his language suggests a tone of familiarity.

C. Invitations. (16.)

110, 111, 112, 523–524, 747, 926–927 (invitation to dine in celebration of a friend's admission to

---

[1] See MILLIGAN'S *Selections*, p. 54.

a class wholly or partially exempt from the poll-tax (ἐπίκρισις)), 1214, 1484–1487, 1579–1580, 1755.

N.B.—(*a*) 110, 523, 1484, 1755 are invitations to dine " at the table of the lord Serapis." But the place of dining differs. In 110 it is the Serapeum ; in 523 a private house.

(*b*) 111, 524, 927, 1579, 1580 are invitations to a wedding-feast, and are formal in character.

(*c*) 112 is an invitation to a birthday festival (cf. also 1214) of a god. In this case the invitation is less formal, being conveyed in a letter couched in friendly terms.

(*d*) in 1485, 1486 the invitation is given for the same day, not, as usually, for the day following.

D. Recommendation. (8.)

292, 746, 787, 1162 (a presbyter, Leon, commends a brother Christian to the priests and deacons of a local church), 1219, 1587, 1663, 1767.

E. Business. (41.)

117, 121, 299, 525, 527, 530, 533, 745, 1061–1062, 1064, 1066, 1068, 1156–1158, 1220, 1479–1480, 1588, 1665, 1667–1669, 1671–1675, 1677, 1756, 1758–1760, 1762, 1765, 1771–1772, 1775–1777.

F. Miscellaneous. (2.)

124 (a schoolboy's exercise), 1213 (question to an oracle).

CHAPTER III

VOCABULARY

THE purpose of this chapter is to set forth in respect to these private letters from Oxyrhynchus the vocabular points of contact with the N.T. and so to assist, in some small degree, in ascertaining how far the vocabulary of the N.T. is akin to that of the vernacular κοινή of the Roman Empire. Hence, attention will be paid in the main only to words found in the N.T. and in these papyri but *not* found in classical literature. Exceptions are made to this rule where some striking resemblance to N.T. language is apparent. The evidence may be conveniently classified under the following heads :—

1. Explanatory parallels to N.T. words and phrases.

O.P.

114, 12
(2/3/A.D.)

ἀπὸ Τῦβι πέρυσι.

" Since Tybi of last year." Cf. 2 Cor. viii. 10 ; ix. 2. DEISSMANN (*B.S.*, p. 221) cites B.U. 531, ii. 1 also. Hence the phrase is not so late as was formerly supposed. The combination of prepositions with adverbs is a common feature of H.G.

A further example is seen in O.P. 528, 9 ἀφ' ὅτε
ἐλουσάμην, " since I last bathed."

O.P.

πάντα ὅσα ἦν καθήκοντα ἐποίησα.

115, 5
(2/A.D.)

" I did everything that was fitting." The
phrase strongly recalls Rom. i. 28. Cf. O.P. 930,
20 ; 939, 17. SOUTER (*Pocket Lexicon*, p.
121) says that τὰ μὴ καθήκοντα (" what is unfitting ")
is " a technical phrase of the Stoic philosophy."
Cf. Acts. xxii. 22.

παρηγορεῖτε οὖν ἑαυτούς.

115, 11
(2/A.D.)

" Comfort, therefore, one another." Cf. the
noun παρηγορία (" comfort ") in Col. iv. 11. LIGHT-
FOOT (*Comm. on Col.*, p. 237) says that the term
is used in medical language in the sense of " allevia-
tion."

ἑαυτούς in the papyri and N.T. (cf. Heb. iii. 13)
sometimes stands for ἀλλήλους. Cf. O.P. 260 (*bis*),
Proleg. p. 87, ROBERTSON, p. 690. It occurs in
juxtaposition to ἀλλήλων in Col. iii. 13.

εἰς λόγον Διονυσίου.

116, 2
(2/A.D.)

" For Dionysius," cf. εἰς λόγον ὑμῶν (Phil. iv. 17).
Other noticeable prepositional phrases with λόγος
in these letters are ἐκ τοῦ ἐμοῦ λόγου, " at my
expense " (525) ; εἰς λόγον τόκου, " on account of
interest " (530) ; εἰς λόγον μου, " on my account "
(1495) ; πρὸ λόγον (= πρὸς λόγον), " properly " (1069,
19, 25) ; cf. 1153, 20 ; and οἱ λόγοι, " the accounts "
(1220). On Phil. iv. 15 PLUMMER (*Comm.*, p. 103)
suggests that Paul is using commercial terms.

O.P. λυπόν (= λοιπόν).

119, 8
(2/3/A.D.)   " Henceforth." It is frequently so used in the Pauline writings : (1) As an introduction to a concluding injunction. Cf. 2 Cor. xiii. 11 ; O.P. 1480, 13. MILLIGAN (*Comm. on 1 Thess.* iv. 1, note) says it does " little more than mark the transition to a new subject as in late Greek." (2) Adverbially, suggesting time (so here and in 2 Tim. iv. 8). λοιπόν is probably more colloquial than τὸ λοιπόν.

119, 10 ἄρρον αὐτόν.
(2/3/A.D.)
" Off with Him." Cf. the cry of the Jews at the crucifixion, John xix. 15 ; cf. also John v. 8 and O.P. 1294, 8 ; cf. Luke xxiii. 18 ; Acts xxi. 36, xxii. 22.

ἀναστατόω.

" I upset," " agitate." Cf. Acts xvii. 6, xxi. 38 ; Gal. v. 12. In *B.G.U.* 1079, 20 (A.D. 41) the verb occurs with the meaning " to drive out." GRIMM'S assertion (*Greek-English Lexicon*, p. 42), " a verb found nowhere in profane authors," is thus refuted. DEISSMANN (*L.A.E.*, p. 81) cites several instances of the word in the secular sense.

291, 8 ἀπαιτέω.
(A.D. 25)
Common in the sense of " demanding payment." Cf. O.P. 298, 19 ; 939, 16 ; 1157, 15 ; Luke vi. 30, xii. 20. In Luke xii. 20 we find the idiomatic impersonal plural. Cf. *M.M.*, p. 52. In Aramaic, and consequently in Synoptic translations, the passive was often replaced by an impersonal third plural active. (See *Proleg.*, p. 163, note.)

ἔχειν αὐτὸν συνεσταμένον.

O.P.
292, 6
(A.D. 25)

" To treat him as one recommended to you." A similar construction is found in Luke xiv. 18–19, which some scholars interpret as a Latinism (= habe me excusatum). See H. McLachlan (*St. Luke, the Man and His Work*, p. 49). Cf. O.P. 787, 2 ; Rom. xvi. 1.

ἐγὼ δὲ βιάζομαι ὑπὸ φίλων.

294, 16
(A.D. 22)

" I am pressed by my friends." Cf. Matt. xi. 12 (= Luke xvi. 16). In *M.M.*, p. 109, it is argued that this instance shows that βιάζεται in Matt. xi. 12 can be passive, " as all the ancient versions assume." On the other hand, Deissmann (*B.S.*, p. 258) holds that the instance is an example of the use of the absolute middle. Robertson (*Gram.*, p. 816) points out that it is often difficult to tell whether a verb is middle or passive.

ἀσπάζεταί σε Σαραπίων καὶ πάντες οἱ παρ᾽ ἡμῶν.

298 37
(1/A.D.)

" Serapion, with all at his house, salutes you." οἱ παρ᾽ αὐτοῦ is very frequent in the papyri denoting " his representatives." Cf. O.P. 935, 14. Mark iii. 21, where the context seems to demand the meaning " his family," has hitherto been hard to parallel. The present confirmatory instance may be added to those cited by Moulton (*Proleg.*, pp. 106–107) and by Witkowski (*E.P.G.*, pp. 96, 119). The latter gives to the phrase the meanings " nostri, propinqui, familiares, amici." Cf. O.P. 805, 7. It would not be an unnatural extension of meaning to pass from " representatives " to " relatives." Robertson (*Gram.*, p. 615) quotes Luke x. 7, τὰ παρ᾽ αὐτῶν, " one's resources or property."

O.P.   For ἀσπάζεται see note under " Epistolary
Phrases," Chapter V, p. 116 f.

523, 3
(2/A.D.)   ἐν τοῖς Κλαυδίου Σαραπίωνος.

" At the house of Claudius Sarapion," an interesting attestation of the R.V. rendering of Luke ii.
49.   Cf. O.P. 1215, 4, εἰς τὸ Σατύρου, " to the house
of Satyrus."

525, 3
(2/A.D.)   βαροῦμαι δι' αὐτόν.

" I am burdened on account of it."   Cf. Luke ix.
32 (βεβαρημένοι ὕπνῳ) and O.P. 939, 23.   The
metaphorical use (as in this instance) is seen in
2 Cor. i. 8, v. 4.   It is noteworthy that the verb
is found in N.T. only in the passive.   M.M. (p. 103)
says, "instances of the active are late in appearing."   To O.P. 1159, 2, which is there quoted as
an instance of the active, may be added O.P. 1224.

The gradual displacement of the classical βαρύνω
by βαρέω is of interest.   βαρύνω is common in the
LXX (βαρέω only in Exod. vii. 14 ; 2 Macc. xiii. 9),
but is not found in N.T. except in the compound
in Mark xiv. 40 and as a variant in Luke xxi. 34.
Cf. O.P. 298, 26 ; Wisd. ii. 4.

The sense of " financial burdening " which the
term commonly carries in the papyri illustrates
1 Tim. v. 16.

530, 8–10   ἐπὶ μάτη[ν δὲ τῶι τοῦ Παυσιρίωνος τοσοῦτον χρόνον
(2/A.D.)   προσκαρτερ[ῶ.

" I have been so long engaged with Pausirion's
business to no purpose."   The Biblical use of the
verb προσκαρτερῶ is interesting :—

(a) " to be of good heart." Cf. LXX (Num. xiii. 21 ; Tobit v. 8).

(b) " to continue steadfastly in." Cf. Acts. i. 14, κ.τ.λ.

(c) " to attend upon " or " wait on " (used in connection with " a little boat " in Mark iii. 9).

MILLIGAN (*Select.*, p. 73) says " the verb is also frequent in the papyri of ' attending ' a court."

ὀψαρία.

531, 18 (2/A.D.)

" Dainties." In N.T. only in John vi. 9–11, xxi. 9 ff. and 13. In both cases it is found in conjunction with ἄρτος (" bread "). ὀψάριον and ὀψώνιον are both diminutives of ὄψον (" relish "). Cf. O.P. 744, 7. ὀψαρίδιον, (" a little fish "), a double diminutive of ὀψάριον is found in O.P. 1067, 28, and ταγαρίδια, " stores," (from τάγη) in 1158, 12. An increase in the use of diminutives is a noticeable feature of the κοινή.

ἐν τῷ δέ με περισπᾶσθαι.

743, 36 (B.C. 2)

" Owing to my worries "—the very word used of Martha in Luke x. 40. Thus the N.T. usage of the word in its metaphorical sense of " distraction " is seen to be quite normal κοινή.

For the supposed Hebraism of this particular infinitive construction see Chapter IV (p. 80).

πολιτάρχος, " politarch."

745, 4 (A.D. 1)

In the N.T. the form is πολιτάρχης (Acts. xvii. 6, 8). The word found thus in the papyri and inscriptions tends to confirm Luke's historical

O.P.   accuracy. It was a special term applied to the magistrates of Thessalonica. MILLIGAN (*Epp. to Thess.*, p. xxiii), following BURTON, states that the office of politarch was not in all probability confined to Thessalonica, and the present instance supports BURTON's view. G.H. in *O.P.*, vol. iv. p. 245, say " the title is new in Egyptian papyri."

745, 2   χειρόγραφον, " a bond."
(1/A.D.)

Only once in N.T. (Col. ii. 14). ROBERTSON (*Gram.*, p. 168) locates the word in Polyb., Dion., Hal., Tob., Plut., Artem. It is common in the papyri. The present instance (cf. also O.P. 1223, 16) may be added to those cited by DEISSMANN (*B.S.*, p. 247) from the Fayûm papyri. It bore the general sense of a written agreement, and also the more technical meaning ' bond,' ' certificate of debt,' which could apparently be cancelled by either washing out (cf. ἐξαλείψας in Col. ii. 14) or writing over. Cf. also B.G.U. 717, 22 ff. (A.D. 149). DEISSMANN (*L.A.E.*, p. 338) suggests that the cancellation was sometimes effected by crossing the bond with the Greek letter Chi (χ). The religious connotation here given to the term is a point of contact between the language of Paul and current legal phraseology.

ROBERTSON (*Gram.*, p. 72) points out that in the κοινή " the number of compound words by juxtaposition is greatly increased," and cites this word as a case in point.

929, 16   ὡς εἶναι ἐπὶ τὸ αὐτὸ ἀριθμῷ ἕξ.
(2/3/A.D.)

" Making the total number six." (G.H.). The frequent occurrences of ἐπὶ τὸ αὐτό in the papyri, especially in accounts, make it clear that it is a phrase of enumeration meaning " together," " in all." So in Luke xvii. 35 ; Acts i. 15, ii. 1, ii. 44, ii. 47 (R.V.m.), iv. 26. Cf. O.P. 1449, 16 and 20.

Luke's use of the phrase in Acts ii. 47 at the end of the sentence is difficult, and it has been suggested that ἐπὶ τὸ αὐτό originally belonged to iii, 1. " Peter and John together," etc. An alternative suggestion that a number has been omitted, viz. " the Lord added to them day by day those that were being saved,—in all," would certainly be in line with the frequent vernacular use of ἐπὶ τὸ αὐτό in arithmetical statements. TORREY renders it in ii, 47 by " very much."

The ἐπί in phrases of this kind has evidently widened and weakened its original suggestion of " motion towards."

For note on ἀριθμῷ see Chapter IV, p. 77 f.

ἡ ἀδελφὴ ἐπὶ τὸ κομψότερον ἐτράπη.

935, 5
(3/A.D.)

" The sister has taken a turn for the better." Cf. P. Tebt. ii. 414, 10, ἐὰν κομψῶς σχῶ (" if I am in good health "), and John iv. 52, κομψότερον ἔσχεν (" he began to mend ").

ἀγωνία, " anxiety."

939, 12
(4/A.D.)

Cf. Luke xxii. 44. The correlative verb ἀγωνιῶ is very common in these private letters (cf. 744, 4 and 14), especially in an exhortation not to " worry."

αὐτόπτης.

1154, 8
(1/A.D.)

" Eye-witness." Once only in N.T. (Luke i. 2).

O.P.
1158, 3
(3/A.D.)

ὁλοκληρεῖν, " to be prosperous."

Luke uses the substantive in Acts iii. 16, and it occurs also in Plutarch. The term may have a medical flavour, ' health.' Cf. O.P. 1770, 8, ὁλοκληροῦμεν.

1158, 26
(3/A.D.)

κάπηλος.

" Shopkeeper," especially an " innkeeper." The verb occurs in 2 Cor. ii. 17. Cf. Isa. i. 22 and Ecclus. xxvi. 29 (LXX) for its depreciatory sense, " trade dishonestly."

1160, 14
(3/4/A.D.)

ἤργηκα.

" I have been idle." The verb is very common in the papyri in the sense of ' playing,' ' being at leisure.' M.M. (p. 73) point out that the term does not necessarily involve blame or shame (as in our ' idle '). Here, for example, it is morally colourless, implying merely ' leisure ' or ' lack of labour.' In the N.T. the verb certainly seems to imply reproof (' idling,' ' dawdling '), and M.M. find confirmation of this signification in the M.Gr. usage of the verb ' delay,' ' come too late.' ἀργέω is found only once in the N.T. (2 Peter ii. 3), but the causative καταργέω is frequent (Rom. iii. 3 al), mainly in the Pauline writings (25 times), " I annul, abolish."

1223, 18
(4/A.D.)

ὁ οἶκος ἡμῶν περιστάσι κοινωνεῖν μέλλει.

" Our house is likely to be brought to a critical pass " (G.H.). Cf. O.P. 905, 4, πρὸς γάμου κοινωνίαν (" for partnership of marriage "). Cf. Acts ii. 42 ; Phil. iv. 15.

ἀναψύχομεν.

" I refresh myself." Cf. 2 Tim. i. 16.
The use of this epistolary first person plural
bears on Paul's possible use of the same. See
MILLIGAN (*Epp. to Thess.*, p. 131 f.). There is often
an interchange of first person singular and first
person plural in the same letter. See below, p. 127.

παραμυθία, " consolation."

Once only in N.T. (1 Cor. xiv. 3). The verb
occurs in O.P. 939, 26. It is to be noted that as
παραμυθία is collocated with παράκλησις in 1 Cor.
xiv. 3 (cf. Phil. ii. 1), so also are their respective
verbs in 1 Thess. ii. 11, v. 14. παραμύθιον occurs
in Wisd. iii. 18, " consolation."

ἀναβολή.

" Delay." Cf. Acts xxv. 17. *M.M.* (p. 30) say
" the word is used with a large variety of meanings," e.g. in P. Goodsp. Cairo 15, 9 (A.D. 362)
the same phrase as in Acts xxv. 17 occurs, τήν
ἀναβ . πεποιημαι (plus the article), but bearing the
sense " to make an embankment."

ἐνοχλεῖς μοι.

" You are worrying me." Cf. Luke vi. 18 ;
Heb. xii. 15.

πεπλήρωσα αὐτόν (cf. πεπλήρωκα in line 6).

" I have settled his account " (referring to an
outstanding debt). The verb apparently carries
the meaning here ' to pay (a person)'. It has
been suggested by C. H. DODD (Art. in the
Expositor, April 1918) that Phil. iv. 15–18 may

O.P. be similarly translated : ἀπέχω δὲ πάντα . . .
πεπλήρωμαι, ' I have received payment ' . . . ' my
account is settled.' The collocation of various
commercial terms in the context (εἰς λόγον δόσεως
καὶ λήψεως ; καρπός) lends weight to the plea.
If such be the force of the verb, Paul is not improbably making use, in semi-humorous vein, of
a commercial metaphor to allude to the delicate
matter of receiving gifts from his converts.
MOFFATT (The N.T. : A New Translation)—in loco—
appears to take this view of the passage. Cf. also
PLUMMER (Comm. on Phil., p. 103). Cf. O.P. 114, 3,
πεπλήρωκα τὸν τόκον (" I have paid the interest ") ;
1773, 31, καὶ πλήρωσον αὐτούς (" and pay them ").

1492, 15 θάρρει.
(late
3/A.D.)   " Be of good courage." Cf. the N.T. form θάρσει
(Mark x. 49 ; Matt. ix. 2 and 22 ; Acts xxiii. 11),
and θαρρέω in 2 Cor. v. 6, 8. Cf. O.P. 1491, 3 ;
θαρρῶ, ' I am confident,' 1665, 11 ; and θαρρείτω in
1587, 19. See below, p. 95.

1664, 6 ἡμῶν ἡ ἡλικία.
(3/A.D.)   " Our youth," as often in N.T. except Luke xix.
3, where it means ' stature.' The N.T. usage is
the ordinary vernacular sense, " full age."

1679, 6 μὴ μετεωρίζου.
(3/A.D.)   " Do not be anxious." Cf. Luke xii. 29.

2. Words used in an Extended or Distinctive Sense.

Under this section are included (a) N.T. words
of supposed special or ' Biblical ' meaning which

are found in these papyri bearing the same signification, and which are accordingly to be regarded
as samples of popular Greek. (*b*) Words common
to these papyri and the N.T., but which show, in
the latter, a deepened or enriched meaning. Many
words used in a popular sense take on, in the
hands of the N.T. writers, a distinctly religious
connotation. The formative power of Christianity
in the sphere of language lies mainly in this direction, that is, it shows itself not so much in the
coining of new words (though, as DEISSMANN, in
his *B.S.*, p. 65, note, says : " It is, of course, true
that the language of the early Christians contained a series of religious terms peculiar to itself,
some of which it formed for the first time ") as
in the deepening of the existent secular vocabulary.
Common terms were clothed with a deeper spiritual
significance (see HUDDILSTON'S *Essentials of N.T.
Greek*, p. xx).

ἐρωτάω.

"I invite." In classical Greek ἐρωτάω = inter-
rogo ; in the Pauline writings ἐρωτάω = rogo,
' I request,' ' beseech.' Cf. 1 Thess. v. 12 ; 2 Thess.
ii. 1 ; Phil. iv. 3 ; O.P. 292, 7 ; 294, 28 ; 744, 6 ;
523, 1 ; 524, 1. The fact that this sense of ἐρωτάω
is found frequently in the κοινή puts out of court
the view that the N.T. usage of the verb was due
to the influence of the Hebrew שָׁאַל. DEISSMANN
(*B.S.*, p. 195) cites several Fayûm papyri yielding
ἐρωτάω = ' I beg.' It is, as he says, " popular
Greek." The construction in 1 Thess. iv. 1
(ἐρωτῶμεν . . . ἵνα) is paralleled in O.P. 744, 14.
(1/B.C.).

O.P.

118, 32
(late
3/A.D.)

τῇ παρουσίᾳ αὐτοῦ.

" His presence." Cf. Phil. ii. 12 ; O.P. 1668, 25.
In classical Greek the word means (a) ' presence,'
(b) ' arrival.' In the LXX (Judith, x. 18 ; 2 Macc.
viii. 12 ; xv. 21 ; 3 Macc. iii. 17) it bears a general
untechnical sense. In the papyri παρουσία has
become a technical term denoting the visit of a
royal personage. This characteristically Pauline
word thus receives illumination. The early Christians found words like παρουσία in common currency,
and, as MILLIGAN (Select., p. xxx) remarks, they
gave them " the deeper and more spiritual sense
with which the N.T. writings have made us
familiar." The same scholar has an elaborate
study of the term in his Epistles to the Thess.
(p. 145 ff.), in which he shows that the word was
most appropriate in emphasising the nearness and
certainty of the Second Coming. Cf. Matt. xxiv. 3.

It is noteworthy that regal and legal phraseology
often came to be employed to express religious
conceptions. Cf. L.A.E., p. 372 f.

294, 11
(A.D. 22)

εἰ ταῦτα οὕτως ἔχει ἀσφαλῶς.

" Whether these things are certainly so." ἀσφαλῶς
occurs in this specialised sense of ' assuredly '
(rather than the usual sense of ' securely ' or
perhaps as an extension of it) in Wisd. xviii. 6 ;
Acts ii. 36. The substantive (ἀσφαλεία) is rare in
the N.T. (1 Thess. v. 3 ; Luke i. 4 ; Acts v. 23).
In the papyri it bears the technical sense of
' security,' ' bond.'

299, 2
(late
1/A.D.)

ἀραβών, " earnest-money."

Cf. O.P. 1673, 21. The N.T. sense of the word

(2 Cor. i. 22, v. 5 ; Eph. i. 14) as a part given in
advance (in guarantee of what is to follow) is
verified in the papyri. *M.M.* (p. 79) give ample
instances including the present one in which a
certain Horus gives eight drachmæ to a mouse-
catcher as earnest-money. The word is found in
the LXX only once (Gen. xxxviii. 17 ff.), and
means ' pledge.' ROBERTSON (*Gram.*, p. 95)
includes ἀρραβών (= עֵרָבוֹן) in his list of words
which are " known to be Hebrew and not Aramaic."
The word is found in classical Greek.

For the spelling of ἀρραβών see note in
Chapter IV, p. 94.

κεφάλαιον.

" Capital " (as against " interest "). Cf. Acts xxii.
28 (' sum of money '). For a parallel to Heb. viii.
1 (' chief point ') cf. O.P. 67, 18 (A.D. 338).
ἐπικεφάλαιον (' poll-tax ') is found in O.P. 1157, 14,
and is a *var. lectio* in Mark xii. 14, where it is
read for κῆνσον by D., *al.*

ὑπὸ κακοῦ συνειδότος κατεχόμενος.

" Being oppressed by an evil conscience." συνειδός
is frequent in Philo and Chrysostom. The N.T.
form is συνείδησις (Rom. ii. 15, ix. 1 ; 1 Pet. ii.
19 ; Heb. ix. 9 κ.τ.λ.) It occurs 31 times and is
largely Pauline. (John viii. 9, καὶ ὑπὸ τῆς . κ.τ.λ., is
very slenderly supported.) Cf. especially Wisd.
xvii. 11, πονηρία . . . συνεχομένη τῇ συνειδήσει.
The word is a Greek conception (Menander has
" for all of us, conscience is God "). MILLIGAN
(*N.T.D.*, p. 57) cites this word as an instance of
Paul's use, on occasion, of current philosophic

O.P.

526, 8
(2/A.D.)

532, 22
(2/A.D.)

O.P.

language. H. A. A. KENNEDY (*St. Paul and the Mystery-Religions*, pp. 158–159) says that the term συνείδησις belongs to Greek (popular) philosophy, but shows that the specifically Christian and Jewish usage of this striking term in the sense of our conception of ' conscience ' or personal moral responsibility has no analogy in Stoicism. This term may therefore be accounted another word to which Paul's religious genius has lent large enrichment.

On κατέχω MILLIGAN (*Epp. to Thess.*, p. 155 f.) has an informing note. He shows that it means in those Epistles (*a*) ' hold fast,' (*b*) ' hold back.' Akin to (*b*) is the rendering suggested by DEISS-MANN (*L.A.E.*, p. 305, note 5), ' I cripple.' Cf. " the restraining power " (ὁ κατέχων) of 2 Thess. ii. 7, viz. the Roman law personified in the emperors. 2 Cor. vi. 10 would seem to lean to the meaning ' hold fast.' MILLIGAN quotes this example from O.P. 532, 22 as an instance of the slightly meta-phorical use of the word. In Luke xiv. 9, O.P. 118, 11 (late 3/A.D.) it evidently means ' take possession of,' and in O.P. 1483, 18 (2/3/A.D.) it bears " the closely related meaning " of ' seize ' (see *M.M.*, p. 336). For the commonest signifi-cance of the verb ' hold back,' ' detain,' cf. 2 Thess. ii. 7 ; Luke iv. 42 ; Rom. i. 18 ; Philem. 13 ; and O.P. 527, 7 (2/3/A.D.), ἐγὼ αὐτὸν κατέχω, " I am detaining him."

743, 22
(2 B.C.)

ἐγὼ ὅλος διαπονοῦμαι.

" I am quite upset." So used in Acts iv. 2 ; xvi. 18. The verb usually suggests ' working laboriously.'

δέδωκα ἐπιτροπήν.

" I have entrusted the care of," etc. In Acts xxvi. 12 the word is similarly used of that which is entrusted, ' commission ' (R.V.).

ἀδελφή, " sister."

This term and its correlative ἀδελφός are used in reference to (a) family kinship. ἀδελφός is employed loosely to mean now ' brother ' and now ' husband.' So ἀδελφή = 'wife' and 'sister.' On the other hand, DEISSMANN (L.A.E., p. 154, note 4) says that marriage between brother and sister was not uncommon in Egypt. Probably the terms were used by husband and wife as a mark of familiarity. LETRONNE (see M.M., p. 9) states that the Ptolemies called their wives ἀδελφαί even when they were not actually their sisters. MILLIGAN (Select., p. 9) speaks of the practice as " a well-established Egyptian usage." Of the present instance WITKOWSKI (E.P.G., p. 131) remarks : " Alis fuit Hilarionis soror et, ut videtur, etiam uxor (sic et Gf-H)." ἀδελφός may be used of a near friend, as in P. Par. 48, 3 (E.P.G., p. 66). Cf. in this respect O.P. 1158, 1, where ἀδελφός = φίλος, and 1219, 2, where some one is referred to as ' our son ' who is not such in actuality. πατήρ and μήτηρ, used very loosely and freely in O.P. 1296, 8, 15, 18 ; 1665, 2 ; 1678, 19 ff., point in the same direction.

(b) Membership in the same religious community, e.g. in the Serapeum at Memphis. Hence, as SOUTER (Pocket Lexicon, p. 6) remarks, this usage, though " characteristic of Jewish literature, is not confined to it." It penetrated the N.T.

O.P.

through Judaism. Cf. 1 Cor. ix. 5 ; 1 Thess. i. 4 (it occurs 21 times in 1 and 2 Thess.). It is by no means easy to determine in passages like Rom. xvi. 23 ; 2 Cor. viii. 18 ; xii. 18, whether the reference is primarily to family relationship or religious brotherhood.

744, 10
(1 B.C.)

ἔκβαλε.

" Cast it out " (an infant). Cf. Gal. iv. 30. Luke has τοῦ ποιεῖν ἔκθετα, "to cast out" (Acts vii. 19).

938, 2
(3/4/A.D.)

ἐνεδρεύσας τὰς τροφὰς.

" Having intercepted the corn." In N.T. the verb is Lucan (Luke xi. 54 ; Acts xxiii. 21) and bears the same sense of ' laying a trap.' Cf. Wisd. ii. 12. In other papyri it extends its meaning to ' defraud.' Cf. O.P. 237, 36 ; 484, 10. Cf. the substantive ἐνέδρα in Acts xxv. 3, ' lying in wait.'

939, 20
(4/A.D.)

σωτηρία, " safety."

The word occurs regularly in the κοινή in the sense of ' health ' or ' well-being.' Cf. O.P. 1666, 19. The N.T. has deepened its meaning. See note by SANDAY AND HEADLAM (Rom., p. 23 f.). In Acts xxvii. 34, Heb. xi. 7, it means ' welfare,' ' safety.'

939, 25
(4/A.D.)

ἀνακαθεσθεῖσα.

" In that she has sat up," a medical term found in Luke vii. 15, Acts ix. 40.

939, 28
(4/A.D.)

ἄφιξις.

Used here in its ordinary meaning ' arrival ' (ἀφικνέομαι). It is very difficult to parallel its usage in Acts xx. 29, where the sense clearly demands 'departure.' "Removal from among you" (not "death") would seem to be KNOWLING's rendering (*E.G.T.*, Acts, p. 437). The nearest parallel is Josephus, *Antiq.*, ii. 18, but, as *M.M.* (p. 98) point out, the word is found in Josephus, *Apion*, i. 18, bearing its usual meaning of 'arrival.' BLASS (*Gram.*, p. 5) argued that Luke (in Acts xx. 29) had misused the word. But Josephus' use of the noun in the sense of 'departure' shows at least that the word was taking on a certain elasticity of meaning.

χρεία.

1063, 8
(2/3/A.D.)

"Office." Cf. 1 Macc. xii. 45 ; 2 Macc. vii. 24 ; Judith xii. 10 ; Acts vi. 3. J. ARM. ROBINSON (*Comm. on Eph.*, p. 193) says that the word means (*a*) need, (*b*) an occasion of need, (*c*) the matter in hand.

οἱ ἐνέγκαντες.

1068, 9
(2/3/A.D.)

"The bearers" (at a funeral). Cf. the use of ἐξενέγκαντες in Acts v. 6, 10.

ἐντυγχάνω κατ' αὐτοῦ.

1160, 21
(3/4/A.D.)

"I will petition against him." Cf. Rom. xi. 2. The present example may be added to those instances of ἐντυγχάνω κατά given by *M.M.*, p. 219. Cf. further O.P. 533, 25 (2/3/A.D.), ἐνέτυχον τῷ διοικητῇ ἕνεκα τῆς προσόδου ("I petitioned the dioecetes about the revenue"). DEISSMANN (*B.S.*, pp. 121-122) states that the noun ἔντευξις was familiar in technical language in Egypt connoting petitionary prayer. "The verb ἐντυγχάνω has the

O.P.   corresponding technical meaning." Cf. Heb. vii.
25 ; Rom. viii. 27, 34.

1217, 6   ὑγιαίνοντά σε καὶ εὖ διάγοντα.
(3/A.D.)

" In health and prosperity." For this derived
sense of διάγω cf. 1 Tim. ii. 2 ; Titus iii. 3 ; O.P.
1664, 2, the reference being to one's general condition or circumstance. Cf. O.P. 1679, 17, καλῶς
διάγομεν, " we are well." It occurs in the usual
sense of ' staying ' in a place in O.P. 1663, 4.
In O.P. 1664, 16–17 both shades of meaning are
found in conjunction.

1220, 20   οὐδὲν ἠφάνισεν ὁ ἱπποποτάμις.
(3/A.D.)

" The hippopotamus has destroyed nothing." The
verb ἀφανίζω is here used in its secondary sense of
' disfigure,' ' destroy.' Cf. Matt. vi. 16, where the
face is ' disfigured ' through being left unwashed.

1223, 22   σπεκουλάτωρ, " speculator."
(4/A.D.)

Cf. Mark vi. 27 ; O.P. 1193 (an order from a
' speculator ') ; 1214, 2. Thus HICKIE's statement
(Greek-Eng. Lexicon, p. 176), " it is an utterly
un-Greek word," needs qualification. ROBERTSON
(Gram., p. 109) notes the word as a Latinism.

1479, 8   κεχρημάτικεν Σαβεῖνος.
(late
1/A.D.)

" Sabinus has been acting in the business."
The verb χρηματίζω has two apparently unrelated
meanings in N.T. :—

(1) ' to be called ' (Acts xi. 26 ; Rom. vii. 3).
Probably derived from χρῆμα = ' affairs.' Hence
the verb means ' to trade as,' then ' to get a name

from one's employment or conduct,' and so ' to be called.'

(2) ' to be warned ' (Matt. ii. 12, 22 ; Heb. viii. 5). Derives from χράω = ' to give an oracular response.' DEISSMANN (*B.S.*, p. 122) asserts that χρηματίζειν is correlative to ἐντυγχάνειν in petitions and signifies the king's ' giving an answer.' The word is used in Job xl. 3 (LXX) and Matt. ii. 12 of a Divine command.

ᾧ ἐὰν δοκιμάσῃς.

" To whomsoever you approve." The papyri evidence shows that the verb developed its meaning from ' testing ' to ' approving.' *M.M.*, p. 167, say : " In the inscriptions, indeed, the verb is almost a term. techn. for passing as fit for a public office." Cf. O.P. 928, 7 (2/3/A.D.), where the meaning borders on δοκεῖν. In O.P. 533, 24 (2/3/A.D.) the verb used is, apparently, δοκιμάω. Cf. Rom. ii. 18 ; Phil. i. 10 ; 1 Thess. ii. 4 (MILLIGAN'S note).

εὐφρανθῆναι σὺν αὐτῷ,

" To rejoice with him " (referring to a birthday festival), recalls Luke's special connotation of the verb suggesting the revelry of feasting. Cf. Luke xii. 19, xv. 23, xvi. 19.

3. Current Phrases or Formulæ.

αὔριον, ἥτις ἐστὶν ιε̄.

" To-morrow, which is the fifteenth." A common formula in letters of invitation. Cf. O.P. 524, 3 ; 1025, 16. The same order of the words is observable in Matt. xxvii. 62, but in O.P. 927, 3

O.P. we have ἥτις ἐστὶν αὔριον κθ (" to-morrow the twenty-ninth ").

113, 27
(2/A.D.)

ἵνα συνάρωμαι αὐτῶι λόγον.

" That I may settle accounts with him."
THAYER-GRIMM'S assertion (*Lexicon*, p. 381) that
this is " an expression not found in Greek authors "
is thus disproved. The phrase (in the active)
occurs in B.G.U. III, 775, 19 (2/A.D.), and in
Matt. xviii. 23, xxv. 19. MOULTON (*Proleg.*, p. 160)
says the middle is " more classical in spirit."
DEISSMANN (*L.A.E.*, p. 119) cites an ostracon of
A.D. 214 where the phrase ἄχρι λόγου συνάρσεως
(" till the reckoning of the account ") occurs. It
is noteworthy that in the two relevant N.T.
passages συνᾶραι is followed by μετά and the
genitive rather than (as here) by the dative.
μετά has ousted σύν in M.Gr.

294, 23
(A.D. 22)

δοῦναι εἰκανὸν.

" To give security." Cf. Acts xvii. 9, where the
corresponding phrase λαμβάνειν τὸ ἱκανὸν (" to
take security ") is used, which MILLIGAN (*Epp. to
Thess.*, p. xxix, 2) shows to be paralleled in an
inscription, O.G.I.S. 484, 50 (2/A.D.). In the N.T.
ἱκανός is typically Lucan. MOULTON (*Proleg.*,
p. 20), whilst sceptical of the extent of Latin
influence on the κοινή, allows it in such phrases as
these, which, he says, are " literally translated."
The Latinising influence in the N.T. appears in
a greater degree in the lexical than in the grammatical realm.

ἱκανός, referring to the *word* of persons, occurs
in O.P. 1672, 15.

οἱ πράκτορες.

"Collectors of revenue." Cf. O.P. 533, 22 (πρακτορεία), and Luke xii. 58, where a subordinate officer of the court is apparently referred to. It is suggestive to note the juxtaposition of ἀντίδικος and πράκτωρ in both O.P. 533 and Luke xii. 58. It may be that Luke is here using the technical terminology of legal affairs. See DEISSMANN (B.S., p. 154).

δὸς ἐργασίαν.

"Give your attention to it" (G.H.). The phrase occurs in Luke xii. 58. This expression has been accounted a Latinism (= operam do). DEISSMANN (L.A.E., p. 117), however, states that it is found in an inscription dated 81 B.C. It is also met with in an unpublished P. Bremen, No. 18 (A.D. 118). These facts, together with its occurrence in the present vulgar papyrus, suggest that it was one of many standing phrases in the contemporary language which found their way into the N.T.

διαστολὰς δεδώκειν.

"To give instructions." The same phrase occurs in 1 Cor. xiv. 7, but is rendered in the R.V. "if they give not a distinction (in the sounds)." Cf. Exod. viii. 23, δώσω διαστολὴν, "I will put a division" (R.V.). The N.T. connotation of the word has not yet been adequately paralleled in the papyri, where the term seems uniformly to mean 'memorandum' or 'instruction.' It is found in Polybius II, chap, xl, § 5, in the sense of 'distinctness' (in narrative).

O.P.
744, 8
(1/B.C.)

λαβεῖν ὀψώνιον, " to receive a present."

Cf. 2 Cor. xi. 8. SANDAY AND HEADLAM (*Romans*, p. 170) derive ὀψώνιον from ὄψον ('relish') and ὠνέομαι ('buy'). Hence it came to mean (1) wages (in a general sense), " pecunia alimentorum loco data " (WITKOWSKI, *E.P.G.*, p. 132). Cf. O.P. 1295, 14 ; διμήνου ὀψώνιον, " wages for two months." (2) Military pay (stipendia) in particular. So Luke iii. 14 ; 1 Cor. ix. 7. " The word is said to have come in with Menander " (SANDAY AND HEADLAM, *op. cit.*, p. 170), and is found in Polybius.

931, 8
(2/A.D.)

τῶι κρατίστωι ἡγεμόνι.

" His excellency the prefect." G.H. say on this passage that " the fact that the prefect is called κράτιστος, not λαμπρότατος, indicates that the letter was written before the close of the second century." Cf. Luke i. 3 and O.P. 967, 2. Of the primary superlative ending—ιστος, ROBERTSON (*Gram.*, p. 278) says " it was never very widely used and has become extinct in Modern Greek." MOULTON (*Proleg.*, p. 78) discounts its superlative force in Luke i. 3, κράτιστε being " only a title." *M.M.* (p. 358) write : " By the end of the third century the title was applied to persons of less importance, e.g. a ducenarius in P.Oxy. xiv. 1711, 4." Cf. Acts xxiii. 26 ; xiv. 3 ; xxvi. 25.

935, 5
(3/A.D.)

κομψότερον τρέπειν.

" To be on the mend " (after illness) The phrase recalls John iv. 52. Cf. the variant phrase in O.P. 939, 17 (4/A.D.), ὡς δὲ ἐπὶ τὸ ῥᾷον ἔδοξεν τετράφθαι, " as she seems to have taken a turn for the better."

νὴ γὰρ τὴν σὴν σωτηρίαν.

"For by your own safety." This adverbial accusative was a common form of Attic adjuration. Only once in N.T. (1 Cor. xv. 31).

διδόναι λόγον.

"To render an account." Cf. O.P. 1281, 9 ; Rom. xiv. 12. The phrase, together with its kindred form λόγον ἀποδιδόναι (cf. Matt. xii. 36 ; Luke xvi. 2 ; Heb. xiii, 17), seems to have primary reference to future judgment.

οὐχ ἔχεις πρᾶγμα.

"It is not your affair." The term πρᾶγμα may be used generically 'business,' or as DEISSMANN (B.S., p. 233) remarks, in a special forensic sense 'law-suit' (causa). Cf. O.P. 743, 19 ; 1 Cor. vi. 1 ; and 1 Thess. iv. 6 where the word is best interpreted to refer to 'the matter in hand,' i.e. fleshly sins. Its general meaning appears in O.P. 525, 4.

4. Miscellaneous.

δειπνῆσαι εἰς κλείνην τοῦ κυρίου Σαράπιδος.

"To dine at the table of the lord Serapis." Cf. O.P. 523, 2 ; 1 Cor. x. 21. The correspondence in the Pauline language is striking, but it may be, as DEISSMANN (L.A.E., p. 355) points out, nothing more than a case of independent parallelism. Paul's usage may derive from LXX passages like Mal. i. 7, 12 ; Ezek. xliv. 16, xxxix. 20. Cf. 1 Cor. x. 21 ('table of devils') with Isa. lxv. 11 (LXX). See below, p. 133 ff.

O.P.
111, 2
(3/A.D.)

ἐρωτᾶν εἰς γάμους, " to invite to a marriage celebration."

Very common in the papyri. In the N.T. the phrase is invariably καλεῖν εἰς. Cf. John ii. 1 ; Matt. xxii. 3. καλεῖ, however, is found in the invitations of O.P. 747, 926, 927. G.H. (*O.P.*, vol. xii. p. 244) say " it is noticeable that in the course of the third century καλεῖ takes the place of the earlier ἐρωτᾶ." But καλεῖ occurs uniformly in the N.T. which is earlier than the third century. Note, however, Luke vii. 36, xi. 37, where ἐρωτάω may well bear the sense " invite."

117, 14
(2/3/A.D.)

ῥάκη δύο.

" Two strips of cloth." Cf. Mark ii. 21 (= Matt. ix. 16).

528, 5
(2/A.D.)

προσκύνημά ποιέω.

" I do an act of veneration " (on behalf of some one). The phrase is very frequent in the papyri ; Cf. O.P. 936, 4 ; 1070, 8 ; κ.τ.λ. (προσκύνημα does not occur in N.T., but προσκυνέω and προσκυνητής are found, Matt. ii. 2 ; John iv. 23.) προσκύνημα was presumably a technical term in contemporary religious phraseology, ' prayer ' made, as DEISSMANN (*L.A.E.*, p. 163) suggests, at a place of pilgrimage for absent friends and relatives.

531, 14
(2/A.D.)

φαινόλιον.

"Cloak." Cf. 2 Tim. iv. 13. MILLIGAN (*N.T.D.*) p. 20) takes the word to signify a ' book-cover.' Cf O.P. 933, 30. ROBERTSON (*Gram.*, p. 109, includes the word in its variant spelling φελόνης (see note on p. 94 below) as a Latinism (= pænula). A few Latin words and phrases mostly pertaining to government were current in Greek-speaking countries. SWETE (*Comm. on St. Mark*, p. 2) says that the vulgar Greek of the Empire " freely adopted Latin words and some Latin phraseology."

O.P.

μὴ ὄκνι μοι γράφειν.

930, 1
(3/4/A.D.)

" Do not hesitate to write to me." The verb ὀκνέω is found only once in the N.T. (Acts ix. 38, μὴ ὀκνήσῃς διελθεῖν) and is followed by the infinitive as here, " delay not to come on (to us)."

διασώζειν.

939, 8
(4/A.D.)

" To bring safely through (an illness)." It is frequent in the papyri. *M.M.* (p. 154) give several examples. Cf. Matt. xiv. 36 ; Luke vii. 3.

θεοῦ γνῶσις ἀνεφάνη ἅπασιν ἡμῖν.

939, 8
(4/A.D.)

" The knowledge of God appeared to us all." Cf. Luke xix. 11 ; Wisd. ii. 13. See below, p. 153.

συμπόσιον.

1159, 26
(late
3/A.D.)

" Dining-room." Cf. O.P. 1129, 10. Cf. also Mark vi. 39, συμπόσια συμπόσια (' groups of guests '), a construction no longer to be regarded as Hebraistic. See note on τρία τρία on p. 85, below.

ἰδοὺ μὲν ἐγὼ οὐκ ἐμιμησάμην σε.

1295, 3
(2/3/A.D.)

" See, I have not imitated you." The frequent use of ἰδού by N.T. writers is explained by MOULTON (*Proleg.*, p. 11) as due to the fact that

O.P.

it answers to an equivalent interjection in their native speech. The Aramaism of the expression comes in in the *frequency* with which an interjection with this meaning was used in the writer's mother-tongue. MOULTON aptly cites the analogy of the Welshman's " look you " in Shakespeare. That is, the Greek interjection was brought in the N.T. into unusual prominence (over-use) owing to its accidental correspondence to an Aramaic phrase. Cf. O.P. 1066, 5 (3/A.D.) ; 1069, 11 (3/A.D.) ; 1291, 7 (A.D. 30).

1493, 9
(3/4/A.D.)

τούτου οὖν τὴν ἐπιμέλειαν ποιήσω ὡς ἰδίον υἱόν.

" I will indeed take care of him as though he were my own son." The οὖν in this case (cf. the frequent admonition μὴ οὖν ἄλλως ποιήσῃς, " be sure to do this," as in O.P. 294, 14) seems to have an emphatic or intensive sense. MANTEY (Art. in the *Expositor* of September 1921) suggests that the particle may carry the same meaning in passages like John xx. 29–30, " to be sure Jesus did," etc. ; Matt. iii. 8 ; Luke xiv. 34. Cf. 1 Cor. vi. 7 ; Phil. iii. 8.

1581, 5–6
(2/A.D.)

ἐρωτηθείς, ἀδελφέ, Σαραπίωνα μὴ ἀφῇς ἀργεῖν καὶ ῥέμβεσθαι.

" I beg you, brother, not to allow Sarapion to be idle and to gad about." ῥέμβεσθαι is a rare word. The substantive occurs in Wisd. iv. 12 (ῥεμβασμὸς ἐπιθυμίας, ' giddy whirl of desire '). It may be coined from ῥέμβας = ' one who gads about.'

For the sentiment see p. 138.

CHAPTER IV

A. GRAMMAR

THE aim of this chapter is to discover what data may be yielded by these papyri for the fuller understanding of the grammar of the N.T. This field, which was necessarily left largely unexplored by DEISSMANN in his quest of the lexical significance of the new discoveries, has been well trodden by MOULTON, RADERMACHER, and ROBERTSON. MOULTON (*Proleg.*, p. 39) shows that, in both educated and uneducated vernacular, differences show themselves less in grammar than in vocabulary and orthography. " There are few points of grammar in which the N.T. language differs from that which we see in other specimens of Common Greek vernacular, from whatever province derived " (*op. cit.*). The points and parallels of grammatical significance found in reading these private letters may be thus set forth :—

1. Pronouns.

Λάμπωνι μυοθηρευτῇ ἔδωκα αὐτῷ . . . δραχμὰς η.

O.P. 299, 2 (1/A.D.)

" I gave eight drachmæ to Lampon the mouse-catcher." The redundant personal pronoun αὐτῷ

O.P.

is exactly paralleled in Rev. ii. 7. Such redundancy in the oblique cases of personal pronouns is only what may naturally be expected in colloquial speech, but ROBERTSON (*Gram.*, p. 94) claims that its frequency in the N.T. is due to Hebraic influence. Cf. Matt. v. 40, viii. 1, 23 ; Rev. iii. 8 ; O.P. 1067, 5.

1155, 13
(A.D. 104)

ἵνα ἐπίγοις πρὸς τὶ σοί 'στι.

" In order that you may hasten to do what concerns you." τίς for the relative ὅς is found in the more illiterate papyri, in the inscriptions, and also in the N.T. (Mark vi. 36, xiv. 36 ; Matt. x. 19, xv. 32 ; Luke xvii. 8). Cf. Gen. xxxviii. 25 (LXX) and O.P. 1119, 22-23. In O.P. 1160, 16, τὰ is used for ἅ, " a use not uncommon in the papyri " (G.H.).

1679, 10
(3/A.D.)

αὐτὰ γὰρ εἰς ἀμφότερα εἴλιξα.

" For I wrapped them (garments) up together." It is probable, though not conclusively certain from the context, that more than two garments are referred to. If so, this use of ἀμφότεροι in the sense of ' all ' illustrates two out of the fourteen N.T. instances of the word (Acts xix. 16, xxiii. 8), where more than two seem to be intended in each case. *M.M.* (p. 28) say : " KENYON observes, ' ἀμφότεροι = πάντες in late Byzantine Greek . . . and it is possible that colloquially the use existed earlier.' " In the two Lucan passages, RADER-MACHER (*Gram.*, p. 64) leans to the rendering ἀμφότεροι = ' all.'

2. Adverbs, Prepositions, Conjunctions.

μετὰ πάσης δυνάμεως.

O.P.
292, 5
(1/A.D.)

"With all my might." μετά with the genitive to denote *manner* is very common in the κοινή. Cf. 1 Thess. i. 6; O.P. 1682, 7.

ἐν Ἀλεξανδρίᾳ . . . εἰς Ἀλεξάνδριαν.

294, 4, 6
(A.D. 22)

An example of the frequent interchange of εἰς and ἐν in late Greek. In the N.T., whilst ἐν is firmly entrenched, there are clear signs of its displacement by εἰς, a process carried to completion in M.Gr. vernacular (cf. THUMB, *Handbook*, etc., p. 100). Cf. Mark xiii. 16 with Matt. xxiv. 18. Cf. also Matt. xii. 41; Acts, xix. 22, xxv. 4; O.P. 1068, 6; 1160, 25. MOULTON (*Proleg.*, p. 245, note) says "before ἐν disappeared it was often used for εἰς, just as εἰς was for ἐν. Thus in the late gloss at John v. 4; also four times in Tob." Luke's fondness for εἰς where ἐν might be expected is marked in Acts. ROBERTSON (*Gram.*, p. 449) says "it is hazardous to insist always on a clear distinction between εἰς and ἐν, for they are really originally the same word. The point is that by different routes one may reach practically the same place, but the routes are different." This point has a direct bearing upon the exegesis of passages like John i. 18, and of the baptismal formula εἰς τὸ ὄνομα. Care is needed in building theological conclusions upon supposedly sharp distinctions in prepositional usage which does not find adequate support in the contemporary vernacular. Cf. Mark xiii. 9 (εἰς συναγωγὰς) with Matt. x. 17 (ἐν ταῖς κ.τ.λ).

O.P.

743, 29
(2 B.C.)

χάριν τῶν ἐκφορίων, "for the rents."

The relative position of the preposition is note-worthy. In classical writers χάριν generally follows its case. WITKOWSKI (*E.P.G.*, p. 89) says "among Attic writers χάριν is very rarely placed before its genitive, but more frequently so in Polybius and later writers."

In the LXX χάριν sometimes follows but generally precedes its genitive, e.g. 2 Chron. vii. 21 ; 1 Macc. xiii. 6.

In the N.T. the preposition always follows, except in 1 John iii. 12, χάριν τίνος.

In the papyri, as DEISSMANN (*L.A.E.*, p. 178) says, "this prepositional χάριν often stands before its case." So O.P. 934, 14, χάριν τῶν ποτισμῶν ("for the sake of the irrigation ") ; 1067, 4, χάριν τοῦ ἀδελφοῦ ("for your brother's sake"). Cf. O.P. 1296, 6 ; 1583, 6. In O.P. 1068, 21, χάριν follows, but in 1068, 16 it precedes. So also in 1683, 18.

743, 30
(2 B.C.)

καὶ τὰ νῦν ἐπειπέπομφα αὐτὸν κ.τ.λ., "and now I have sent him."

Quite classical usage of τὰ νῦν. So also in 2 Macc. xv. 8 ; Judith ix. 5. τὸ νῦν occurs in 1 Macc. vii. 35 ; Exod. ix. 27. In the N.T. τὰ νῦν is confined to Acts (iv. 29 ; v. 38 ; xvii. 30 ; xx. 32 ; xxvii. 22). It begins a sentence in every case in Acts except in xvii. 30. But there, as in the present instance, it starts a clause or second half of a sentence. Luke's use suggests that the τά is merely rhetorical, employed to secure balance and emphasis. Cf. B.G.U. IV, 1157, 14 (B.C. 10) ; O.P. 8101, 4 ; 161, 4.

3. Cases.

πολλοῖς χρόνοις.

O.P.
112, 8
(3/4/A.D.)

" For a long time." This instrumental use of the dative to indicate time-duration is common in the papyri. Cf. O.P. 936, 51 ; 938, 8 ; 1066, 25 ; Luke viii. 27 ; Rom. xvi. 25 ; Polybius xxxii. 12. McLACHLAN (*St. Luke, the Man and His Work,* p. 38) points out that conversely " the accusative can be used in the common speech to express point of time, as in Acts xx. 16." SOUTER (*Pocket Lexicon,* p. 285), following the R.V. text, takes the phrase as locative in Luke viii. 29, which ROBERT-SON (*Gram.,* p. 543) commends as a test passage in case usage. In such instances the context only can decide as to the relative claims of locative or instrumental dative. Cf. ROBERTSON (*Gram.,* p. 527), and for the locative use cf. O.P. 742, 6, τῇ ἀναβάσει, " on the up journey."

οὐ μὴ γράψω σε ἐπιστολὴν οὔτε λαλῶ σε οὔτε υἰγένω σε.

119, 5
(2/3/A.D.)

" I won't write you a letter or speak to you or say good-bye to you." The use of the accusative (σε) here is not due to illiteracy, but is an indication that the dative was beginning to drop out of currency in the popular language. Cf. O.P. 744, 8.

παράδος ἀριθμῷ αὐτάς.

742, 7
(2 B.C.)

" Deliver a few of them." MOULTON (*Proleg.,* p. 76) characterises this as a curious instrumental dative and an Ionism. WITKOWSKI (*E.P.G.,* p. 128),

O.P.

following WILCKEN, renders it "accurate dinu-
meratos" ("carefully counted"). A parallel is
found in Herodotus vi. 58. Cf. Num. ix. 20;
Ezek. xii. 16 (LXX). THACKERAY (*Gram.*, p. 39)
shows that the usage is "removed from the category of Hebraisms."

744, 6
(1 B.C.)

παρακαλῶ σε ἐπιμελήθητι τῷ παιδίῳ, "I entreat
you to take care of the child."

ἐπιμελέομαι with the dative is rare. MILLIGAN
(*Select.*, p. 32) cites P. Tebt. 58, 62 f. (B.C. 111)
and Xen. Hellen. v. 4, 4. In the N.T. (Luke x.
34 f.; 1 Tim. iii. 5) the word regularly takes the
genitive and so also in the LXX (except 1 Esdras
vi. 26). Cf. O.P. 1154, 4. According to ROBERTSON
(*Gram.*, p. 509) ἐπιμελέομαι occurs with the dative
in the Attic inscriptions. ἐπιμελεία, "attention,"
"care" (Acts xxvii. 3) is said to be a medical
term.

744, 12
(1 B.C.)

πῶς δύναμαί σε ἐπιλαθεῖν;

"How can I forget thee?" For the accusative
after ἐπιλανθάνομαι see Phil. iii. 13; O.P. 1489, 3.
MILLIGAN (*M.M.*, p. 240) says: "The construction with the accusative in Phil. iii. 13, while not
unknown in classical, is amply attested in later
Greek." ἐπιλανθάνομαι takes the genitive in Heb.
vi. 10; xiii. 2.

1162, 5
(4/A.D.)

χαρᾷ χαίρειν, "fullness of joy."

An instance of cognate instrumental. Cf. John
iii. 29, χαρᾷ χαίρει ("rejoiceth greatly").

ὡς τοῦ ἄλλου μηνὸς ἐλεύσομαι.

" As I shall be returning in another month."

1489, 6, 8
(late
3/A.D.)

εἰ δει, ἔρχομαι τῷ ἄλλῳ μηνί.

" If necessary, I am coming in another month."
This interchange of genitive and dative in
temporal expressions illustrates Mark xiii. 35
(ἀλεκτοροφωνίας . . . πρωΐ). Cf. BLASS (Gram.,
p. 311).

4. Tenses.

ἐξ ὧν δώσεις . . . λυτρώσασά μου τὰ ἱμάτια.

530, 14
(2/A.D.)

" Of which you will give . . . and redeem my
clothes." MOULTON (Proleg., p. 132) cites this
example as an instance of the coincident aorist,
and is disposed to explain ἀσπασάμενοι in Acts
xxv. 13 similarly.

ἀπέστειλα διὰ γραμμάτων.

1682, 3
(4/A.D.)

" I am sending by letter," an example of the
common epistolary aorist. Cf. Phil. ii. 25 ; Eph. vi.
22, al.

5. Moods.

ὅρα οὖν μὴ ἄλλως πράξῃς.

" See therefore that you do not act otherwise."
The construction illustrates Matt. xviii. 10 ; 1 Thess.
v. 15.

532, 15
(2/A.D.)

ἵνα τῇ ἀναβάσει αὐτὰς ἄξωμεν, " that we may take
them on the journey up."

742, 6
(2 B.C.)

MOULTON (Proleg., p. 76 note) labels ἄξωμεν a

O.P.   first aorist subj. as against the view of WITKOWSKI (*E.P.G.*, p. 128), who assumes that it is a future subj. or less probably a future indic. Thus examples of the first aorist subj. in the N.T. are paralleled in the papyri. MOULTON (*Camb. Bib. Essays*, p. 485) shows the relevance of such a point for N.T. criticism. He argues that in Luke iii. 17 (= Matt. iii. 12) Luke (and not Matt. as HARNACK in his *Sayings of Jesus*, p. 1 f., advanced) preserves the original in adhering to the aorist infinitive. The original reading in Q was presumably συνάξαι, the vulgar first aorist infinitive. This was altered by Luke (ℵ* B) into συναγαγεῖν (συνάξει, ℵ*). Matt. altered it to the future συνάξει. Hence HARNACK'S view that Luke always emended Q into more stylistic Greek fails of confirmation (see below, p. 166 f.) Luke preserves many vulgar and vernacular forms.

742, 9   ἵνα πάλιν φίλος ἡμεῖν παραδοῖ.
(2 B.C.)
       "That a friend may deliver them again to us." παραδοῖ is aorist subj. (not optative). Cf. ἀποδοῖς in Luke xii. 59 (D). MOULTON (*Proleg.*, p. 55) suggests that the movement towards such forms in -μι verbs is seen in the present subj. διδοῖ after -όω verbs. Cf. O.P. 932, 8, ἵνα ἐπιγνοῖς τὸν ὄνον ("that you may find out the ass"), and cf. ἐπιγνοῖς in Luke i. 4 (ℵ). Cf. also O.P. 1062, 14.

743, 36   ἐν τῷ δέ με περισπᾶσθαι
(2 B.C.)
       "Owing to my worries." The construction ἐν τῷ with the infinitive has been reckoned a 'pure Hebraism.' (So DALMAN in *Words of Jesus*, p. 33). It is found in classical Greek and in Polybius.

It is very frequent in the LXX, and common in Luke (34 times in the Gospel, and 8 times in Acts), expressing contemporaneous action. It is an exact equivalent of the Hebrew infinitive with ּבְ and this fact helps to make the construction more frequent in Greek. So MOULTON (*Proleg.*, p. 14) and ROBERTSON (*Gram.*, p. 95) agrees. The former (*Proleg.*, p. 249, note) puts it in the category of " possible but unidiomatic Greek." Cf. Matt. xiii. 4 (= Luke viii. 5 ; Mark iv. 4) ; Luke viii. 40 ; ix. 36 *al.*

ἐὰν ἦν ἄρσενον ἄφες, " if it is a male, let it alone."

A -ν could be added apparently without any difference to pronunciation. ἦν, therefore, sometimes = ᾖ (subj.). Cf. Gen. vi. 17 (E), ὅσα ἐὰν ἦν. Hence ἦν is not really indic. but a form of the subj. ᾖ. This usage probably led to extensions, so that we find ἐάν with the indic. in 1 Thess. iii. 8 ; Luke xix. 40 ; Acts viii. 31 ; 1 John v. 15 ; Gen. xliv. 30 ; Job xxii. 3. Cf. O.P. 744, 5. ᾖ (subj.) lost the -ι and took on an irrational -ν, which was commonly tacked on to long vowels.

6. Verbal formations and constructions.

χαρίεσαι (= χαριεῖσαι) δὲ μοι τὰ μέγιστα, " you will grant me a very great favour."

The N.T. parallels καυχᾶσαι (Rom. ii. 17, 23 ; 1 Cor. iv. 7) and ὀδυνᾶσαι (Luke xvi. 25) are explained by MOULTON (*Proleg.*, p. 53 f.), following BLASS, as a fresh formation in the κοινή (in the second singular present indic. middle) by analogy with the -σαι in the perfect. Cf. φάγεσαι, πίεσαι

O.P.

in Luke xvii. 8; δύνασαι (Matt. v. 36); κατακαυχᾶσαι (Rom. xi. 18). THACKERAY (*Gram.*, p. 218) compares κτᾶσαι in Sir. 6, 7. ROBERTSON (*Gram.*, p. 340) says "the -σαι form is universal in modern Greek." It is evident, therefore, that the N.T. writers did not hesitate to use flexions, e.g. καυχᾶσαι, which were distinctively Hellenistic and un-Attic.

526, 3
(2/A.D.)

οὐκ ἤμην ἀπαθὴς ἀλόγως σε καταλείπιν.

" I was not so unfeeling as to leave you." This use of the infinitive in a consecutive sense without ὥστε is paralleled in Heb. vi. 10; Acts v. 3; cf. also Luke i. 54, 72.

1067
(3/A.D.)

There are several instances in this letter of the second person singular of the first aorist and perfect ending in -ες (not -ας), e.g. ἀφῆκες (line 5), οἶδες (line 20). Cf. παρείληφες (O.P. 742, 4); δέδωκες (O.P. 903, 30). THACKERAY (*Gram.*, p. 215) states that " these forms clearly did not take root in Egypt." But " in 2/3/A.D. examples begin to accumulate." Cf. Rev. ii. 3, 5; xi. 17 (W.H.). MOULTON (*Proleg.*, p. 52) thinks that in Rev. this ending is a mark of the author's " imperfect Greek." DEISSMANN (*B.S.*, p. 192) cites B.U. 261, where several examples of the -ες ending are found. In John viii. 57 B* has ἑόρακες, and also ἔδωκες in John xvii. 7, 8.

1682, 9
(4/A.D.)

εἰ ἧς ἐπιδημήσασα.

" If you have arrived." ἧς for ἦσθα is common in the κοινή " (G.H.). Both are found in N.T. (Matt. xxv. 21; xxvi. 69).

GRAMMAR 83

καὶ μὴ ἄφιε ἐποικοδομῆσαι.

O.P.
1758, 13
(2/A.D.)

" Do not allow to build over." G.H. say
" similar forms occur in the LXX and N.T. as
Eccles. ii. 18 (ἀφίω), Mark i. 34 (ἤφιε). Cf.
also Mark xi. 16. The disappearance of the -μι
forms in favour of the -ω inflexion (as here, ἀφίω
for ἀφίημι) is a marked feature of later Greek.
Cf. ἀφιέμεν (Luke xi. 4).

7. Miscellaneous.

ἄν = ἐάν (" if ").

119, 8, 14
(2/A.D.)

MOULTON (*Proleg.* p. 43, note 2) suggests that
this form is " a dialectic variant which ultimately
ousted the Attic ἐάν." In the N.T. it is confined
to the Fourth Gospel (John v. 19 ; xii. 32 (W.H.) ;
xiii. 20 ; xvi. 23 ; xx. 23 (*bis*). In M.Gr. vernacular ἄν is used regularly for ' if.' ROBERTSON
(*Gram.*, p 190, note 2) states that ἄν = ἐάν, ' if,'
is rarely found in the papyri also. The present
example may be added to the list. Cf. ἄμ μὴ
(*bis*) = ἐὰν μὴ. Cf. O.P. 121, 9.

ἄμ μὴ πέμψῃς οὐ μὴ φάγω, οὐ μὴ πείνω.

119, 14
(2/A.D.)

" If you don't send, I won't eat, I won't drink."

This double negative (usually followed by an
aorist subj. or future indic.) is best regarded as
an intensification of the simple οὐ. It is found in
1 Cor. viii. 13 ; Gal. v. 16 ; 1 Thess. iv. 15, v. 3,
bearing, as here, the emphatic sense of classical
Greek (' certainly not '). Cf. Isa. xi. 9 (LXX).

O.P.

The origin of the idiom is far from clear. Cf.
GOODWIN (*M.T.*, p. 389 ff.). ROBERTSON (*Gram.*,
p. 1174) is content to accept GILDERSLEEVE'S
suggestion that it was originally οὔ · μή. MOULTON
(*Proleg.*, p. 188) notes that " οὐ μή is rare, and
very emphatic, in the non-literary papyri." That
the present instance is the only case of οὐ μή
we have discovered in our selection from the
Oxyrhynchan private correspondence supports
MOULTON'S judgment. By allowing for Semitic
originals underlying the Logia of the Gospels
and the Apocalypse (the parts of the N.T.
where the locution is specially frequent) he
reduces the occurrence of οὐ μή in the N.T. to
practically the same degree of rarity as in the
papyri. See the full discussion in *Proleg.*,
pp. 187–192.

121, 3–5   εἶπά σοι . . . εἶνα δώσωσιν.
(3/A.D.)

"I said to you . . . that they were to give
them to us." Cf. O.P. 744, 13, ἐρωτῶ σε ἵνα μὴ
ἀγωνιάσῃς ("I beseech you not to worry").
MOULTON (*Proleg.*, p. 208) decides against any
Latinising influence in this ἵνα development,
which he judges to be perfectly natural. Cf.
Matt. iv. 13, xvi. 20; Mark v. 10. THACKERAY'S
view (*Gram.*, p. 20) is that the influence of Latin
on the grammar of the κοινή was but slight. A
supposed Latinism in grammar may prove to be
nothing more than a natural extension of native
Greek usage. So here, ἵνα denotes purport rather
than purpose. The weakened sense of ἵνα is a
characteristic feature of the κοινή.

εἶνα δήσῃ τρία τρία.

O.P.
121, 19
(3/A.D.)

An injunction to tie twigs into bundles of ' three apiece.'   This instance of a distributive raises the question of the extent of Semitic influence in the analogous N.T. examples, Mark vi. 7, 39–40 ; Matt. xiii. 30 (where EPIPHANIUS reads δεσμὰς δεσμὰς) ; Luke x. 1, a mixed distributive.   It was formerly held that these N.T. expressions were ' properly Hebraistic,' since the repetition of a numeral is a characteristically Hebrew way of conveying a distributive idea.   But, apart from classical instances (μίαν μίαν in SOPH. *Frag.* 201, and μυρία μυρία in AESCH. *Persae*, 981), and LXX (Gen. vii. 15 *al.*), the idiom is now paralleled (as here) from the papyri.   Cf. O.P. 886, 19, κατὰ δύο δύο, and 940, 6, μίαν μίαν.   The usage survives in M.Gr. ROBERTSON (*Gram.*, p. 91) says " this idiom has been traced in Greek for 2500 years."   It is therefore no longer tenable, as THUMB and MOULTON have insisted and as BLASS has admitted, that the idiom derives directly from Hebrew usage. DEISSMANN (*L.A.E.*, p. 125, note 1) cites this present case as " one of the numerous coincidences between the popular phraseology of different languages."   But independence of Hebrew influence must not be pressed too far.   The probability is by no means excluded that, whilst the connection of this colloquial Greek expression with Hebrew is fortuitous, it has been reinforced and extended by the similar Hebrew idiom.   ROBERTSON (*Gram.*, p. 284) sums up : " it is a vernacular idiom which was given fresh impetus from the Hebrew idiom." So also BRUGMANN (quoted in MOULTON's *Proleg.*, p. 21 note).

O.P.
292, 12
(1/A.D.)

τὰ ἄριστα πράττων, " prosperity."

Genuine superlatives are very rare in the papyri, and the N.T. ἄριστος is found in the former, but not in the latter. Cf. O.P. 1061, 21. In the papyri documents superlative forms are usually employed in the elative sense, ' very.' Cf. O.P. 292, 9.

294, 15
(1/A.D.)

ἕως ἀκούσω φάσιν, " until I hear word."

In later Greek ἄν was often omitted after temporal particles like ἕως. Cf. 2 Thess. ii. 7. For φάσις, " information by report," cf. O.P. 293, 8 ; 805, 2 ; Acts xxi. 31.

526,10–12
(2/A.D.)

εἰ καὶ μὴ ἀνέβενε ἐγὼ τὸν λόγον μου οὐ παρέβενον.

" Even if he were not going, I should not have broken my word." An instance of the omission of ἄν in the apodosis of a sentence of unfulfilled condition. Cf. O.P. 530, 17 ; Mark xiv. 21 (=Matt. xxvi. 24). In classical writers ἄν was regularly dropped in the apodosis of unfulfilled conditions with phrases like ἔδει, ἐχρῆν, καλὸν ἦν. Cf. Heb. ix. 26. M.M. (p. 29) state that " the fewness of our examples shows that the N.T. omissions of ἄν, practically confined to John, are not normal κοινή grammar, except in clauses where omission was classical." ROBERTSON (Gram., p. 920), however, does not agree. ἄν in such cases is omitted because it is not needed. Cf. John ix. 33 ; Acts xxvi. 32.

527, 2–3
(2/3/A.D.)

περὶ Σερήνου τοῦ γναφέως ὁ συνεργαζόμενος μετὰ Φιλέου.

" Concerning Serenus the fuller who works with Phileas."

Such instances of breach of concord (cf. O.P. 929, 19, where ἐξ ὧν makes a bad concord with Ὀξυρυγχείτην) are not without significance for similar indifference to grammatical agreement found in the Apocalypse (e.g. Rev. i. 5). On this point J. ARM. ROBINSON (*J.T.S.* X, 9) writes : " it is familiarity with a relaxed standard of speech, such as we find often enough in the professional letter-writers who indited the petitions and private correspondence of the peasants of the Fayûm." So THACKERAY (*Gram.*, p. 23) : " in the breach of the rules of concord is seen the widest deviation from classical orthodoxy. The evidence which the LXX affords for a relaxation of the rigorous requirements of Attic Greek in this respect is fully borne out by the contemporary papyri."

ἐν οἷς ἐάν (= οἷς ἄν) σοῦ προσδέηται, " in whatever service he may ask of you."

743, 33
(2 B.C.)

ἐάν for ἄν in relative sentences is very common in the LXX, N.T. (61 times), and papyri of 1/2/A.D. THACKERAY (*Gram.*, p. 68) shows that the predominance of ἐάν over ἄν began as early as 133 B.C. In papyri dated B.C. the proportion of ἐάν to ἄν is 13 to 29 (*Proleg.*, p. 43), but in the second century A.D. it is 76 to 9. In 4/A.D. it declines to 4 to 8, and disappear in 6/A.D. ἐάν, therefore, was specially common for ἄν in 1/2/A.D., and is " a genuine feature of vernacular Greek " (*Proleg.*, p. 42). In M.Gr. ἄν has almost disappeared except in composition. ὡς ἄν in the papyri nearly always means ' when,' and in H.G. it had practically become identical with ὡς. Cf. Phil ii. 23 ;

O.P.   1 Cor. xi. 34 ; Rom. xv. 24. DEISSMANN (*B.S.*, p. 202 f.) has a thorough discussion.

743, 43   ἐπισκοποῦ τοὺς σοὺς πάντε(ς), " look after all your
(2 B.C.)   household."

For πάντας. MOULTON (*Proleg.*, p. 36) notes that the Achaian accusative plural in -ες as a feature of North-West Greek is common in the vernacular. " In the N.T. τέσσαρας never occurs without some excellent authority for τέσσαρες." Cf. John xi. 17 א Δ ; Acts xxvii. 29 ; Rev. ix. 14 א. Cf. Fay. P., 115, 12 (A.D. 101), τοὺς ἐν ὕκῳ πάντες, " all those at home."

930, 4   ἐντεῦθεν ἐλοιπήθην ἐπιγνοῦσα, " it grieved me to
2/3/A.D.)   learn."

The force of ἐπί in compounds is sometimes explained as amplificatory. Thus ἐπίγνωσις = complete knowledge. MOULTON adopts J. ARM. ROBINSON'S view (*Comm. on Eph.*, p. 248 f.) that the word stands for directive knowledge concentrated on some particular object. Cf. Rom. i. 28. MILLIGAN (*M.M.*, p. 236) says that this interpretation of the force of ἐπί is " on the whole borne out by the evidence of the papyri." But H. A. A. KENNEDY (*St. Paul and the Mystery Religions*, p. 172, note) is not convinced. It is true that the directive force of ἐπί is not always strongly marked. Cf. O.P. 930, 14 ; 932, 8.

932, 8   ἐὰν δύνῃ ἀναβῆναι ἵνα ἐπιγνοῖς τὸν ὄνον.
(late
2/A.D.)   " If you can go up to find out the ass, do so."
The apodosis is omitted. Cf. Luke xix. 42 ; Mark viii. 12 ; 2 Thess. ii. 3 f.

οὐ καυχομαι ἐμαυτὸν κ.τ.λ., " I do not boast."   O.P.

An instance of the redundant middle. ROBERT-   1160, 10
SON (*Gram.*, p. 811) says "this idiom (of redundant   (3/4/A.D.)
middle) is found as early as Homer and indicates
a dimness in the force of the middle on the part
of the speaker." Cf. Acts xx. 24 ; Titus ii. 7.
" Most of the examples, however, in the N.T.
occur with verbs which are not found in the
Active " (*op cit.*, p. 811).

ἅψαι αὐτὸν κεῖται.   1297, 13
     (4/A.D.)

" It is meant for you to burn." The N.T. construction is usually κεῖμαι followed by εἰς and
the accusative of a noun, or pronoun. Cf. Luke ii.
34 ; Phil. i. 16 ; 1 Thess. iii. 3.

It is to be noted that κεῖμαι is found only in
the present and imperfect tenses in both the N.T.
and the papyri.

καὶ οὐκέτι φοβός οὐδὲ εἷς ἔνει.   1668, 19–
     20
" There is no longer any fear at all." For the   (3/A.D.)
form ἔνι (= ἔνεστι) cf. Sir. 37, 2 ; 4 Macc.
iv. 22 ; Gal. iii. 28 ; Jas. i. 17 ; O.P. 1218, 5. It
would seem that in the κοινή the form ἔνι is
taking the place of ἐστί to which, as *M.M.* (p. 215)
say, it is " practically equivalent in meaning."
Cf. especially 1 Cor. vi. 5, οὐκ ἔνι ἐν. HORT (*Epistle
of St. James*, p. 30) says it is " the Ionic form of
ἐν, retained in this Attic idiom like πάρα without
the substantive verb."

καὶ σκύληθι καὶ αὐτὸς ἐνθάδε.   1669, 13–
     14
" Do you yourself be at the pains of coming   (3/A.D.)

O.P. here " (Edd.). This use of a passive aorist imperative in a middle sense illustrates Luke's use of
the middle of this verb in Luke vii. 6, μὴ σκύλλου
(" trouble not thyself "), with which the vernacular
μὴ σκ[λ]ύλλε ἑατήν in O.P. 295, 5 may be compared.
Cf. Mark v. 35 ; Luke viii. 49.

1671, 22   γράψον μοι ὅτι ποῦ εὑρίσκομεν.
(3/A.D.)
" Write to me on the question ' where can we
find them ? ' " This is a case of recitative ὅτι
used to introduce a speech reported in direct
discourse, and is almost equivalent to our quotation marks. So also in the N.T. ὅτι is not always
the sign of indirect quotation, e.g. Mark xiv. 14 ;
John x. 36 ; Matt. ix. 18, xxvii. 43. For the
absence of ὅτι see Matt. ix. 22 ; Mark iv. 21, viii. 4.
Cf. O.P. 1682, 9. JANNARIS (Hist. Greek Grammar,
p. 472) enumerates 120 instances of recitative ὅτι
in the N.T.

1675, 14–   ἵνα οὖν καὶ σὺ ἐπιμελῶς χρήσῃ . . .
15
(3/A.D.)   " Do you therefore make careful use " (Edd.).
This abrupt use of ἵνα illustrates Mark v. 23.
ἵνα has lost its telic force, and used with a second
person subj. indicates a request. So in Mark v.
23, "please come and lay your hands on her."
Cf. Eph. v. 33 ; 2 Cor. viii. 7, where, according to
ROBERTSON (Gram., p. 933), " ἵνα seems to be
merely an introductory expletive with a volitive
subjunctive."

1764, 4–5   πολλαὶ ἡμέραι προσκαρτεροῦμεν Φιλέᾳ τῷ μοσχομαγείρῳ.
(3/A.D.)
" We have been waiting for many days for
Phileas the butcher." An instance of the pendent

nominative of time where the accusative would normally be expected. Cf. Mark viii. 2 (= Matt. xv. 32) ; Luke ix. 28. This example may be added to that given by *M.M.* (p. 280).

B. ORTHOGRAPHY

The discovery of papyri dating from the N.T. period has provided a wealth of material upon which surer inductions concerning the orthography of the N.T. may be based. The data to which WESTCOTT and HORT had access in their researches in the field of N.T. orthography were restricted in range. SOUTER (*Text and Canon of the N.T.*, p. 142) gives several points, e.g. aspirated forms, the coalescence of two -ι sounds, -ν ἐφελκυστικόν, etc., which have been illuminated by the new evidence of the papyri. DEISSMANN (*B.S.*, p. 181) is sceptical of the possibility of discovering a N.T. orthography as such, that is, the spelling originally employed by the writers. " In that respect one can, at most, attain to conjectures regarding some particular author " (*op. cit.*, p. 181). At the same time the papyri and the inscriptions render this useful service ; they show " what forms of spelling were possible in the imperial period in Asia Minor, Egypt, etc." Obvious illiteracies need not be regarded, since, as DEISSMANN (*B.S.*, p. 72, note) points out, the orthography of letters and of other private documents is naturally capricious as compared, for example, with that of official documents. The points of orthographical significance which emerge from a

O.P.   reading of the Oxyrhynchus papyri may be set forth as follows. The fact that they derive from one circumscribed source must constantly be borne in mind. Here, as elsewhere, the evidence should be compared with data drawn from wider areas.

1. Vowel variation.

294, 5
(A.D. 22)
ἔμαθον παρά τινων ἁλιέων, " I learned from some fishermen."

ἁλιεύς is frequently found in the Ptolemaic papyri, whereas in the best MSS. of the LXX and the N.T. ἅλεευς is the regular form (Mark i. 17). In the nominative and accusative plural the form is due to "dissimilation instead of contraction" (*Proleg.*, p. 45, and *Gram.*, vol. ii. p. 76). ι and ε commonly interchange in the Attic and Egyptian κοινή when used with λ and ν (see Robertson, (*Gram.*, p. 188).

397
(1/A.D.)
κολλύραι, "eye-salve."

Cf. Rev. iii. 18, where the MSS. read κολλούριον, κολλύριον, κουλλούριον. -ου as an interchange with -υ is rare in Greek. Blass (*Gram.*, p. 22, § 4) says that the -ου form (κολλούριον) is "certainly of Latin origin." Cf. O.P. 1088, 42 (κολλύρια). The papyri vary, as Moulton (*Gram.*, vol. ii. p. 79) shows. Cf. also Rev. i. 5, λύσαντι (א A.C.) and λούσαντι (B.P.), though there a "supposedly easier sense" may account for the variation.

σεατοῦ ἐπιμελοῦ, "take care of yourself." **O.P.**

For σεαυτοῦ. cf. ἑατον for ἑαυτόν, e.g. O.P. 295, 5
MOULTON (*Proleg.*, p. 47) says "the less educated
papyri writers very frequently use ᾱ for αυ, before
consonants, from 2/B.C. onwards." MAYOR'S suggestion (*Expositor* VI, x. 289) that ἀκαταπάστους in
2 Pet. ii. 14 (AB) may be thus explained is not
improbable.

743, 43
(2 B.C.)

πλῆρος, "full amount."

For πλῆρες. -ο is interchangeable with -ε.
Cf. O.P. 1682, 10, εὐθυμέτεροι ; 1757, 14, ἀβαρός.
Some MSS. of the N.T. have ὀλοθρεύω and ὀλεθρεύω
(ROBERTSON, *Gram.*, p. 189). Cf. Heb. xi. 28 ; 1 Cor.
x. 10 ; Acts iii. 23. HORT (*Notes on Orthography*,
p. 152) accepts the -ε form in the last passage.

1670, 13
(3/A.D.)

2. Consonantal variation.

κιτών = χιτών, "tunic."

KRETSCHMER gives this form as an Ionic factor
in the κοινή. It does not occur in the N.T. MSS.
with the exception of *B** in Mark xiv. 63 (κιτῶνας).
The form χιτών occurs in O.P. 114, 6. MAYSER
(*Grammatik*, p. 41) says the word is Semitic in
origin.

113, 8
(2/A.D.)

δερματικομαφόρτιν, "casket (?)."

-ρ used for -λ. THACKERAY (*Gram.*, p. 107) states
that in the vulgar language -ρ replaces -λ,
especially before consonants. Cf. O.P. 1273, 12.
Cf. the Latin ' flageilum ' dissimilated to φραγέλλιον.
Cf. O.P 242, 12 (77 A.D.) λαύλας (= λαύρας,

114, 5
(2/3/A.D.)

O.P.   " lanes ") ; Luke vi. 41 (W), κάλφος = κάρφος (" a chip of wood ").

299, 2
(late
1/A.D.)   ἀραβῶνα, " earnest-money."

According to Souter (*Text and Canon*, p. 143) ἀρραβών and ἀραβών in Egyptian papyri " are about equally frequent." Hence Westcott's and Hort's assertion that ἀραβών was a reading " only Western " is qualified. They read, following B.C.D. vs, אּ. A.L. ἀρραβῶνα in 2 Cor. i. 22. The word is of Semitic origin (though Dr. D. Smith, in his *Life and Letters of St. Paul*, p. 349, holds that it was originally a Phœnician word and was borrowed by the Hebrews, Greeks and Romans. So also J. Arm. Robinson in his *Comm. on Ephesians*, p. 147. In Paul's day it was a common business term which he enlisted in the service of the Gospel). Deissmann (*B.S.*, p. 183) does not accept the view of Winer-Schmiedel that the Semitic origin of the word establishes the form ἀρραβών. Thackeray (*Gram.*, p. 119) holds that ἀρραβών, read in Gen. xxxviii. 17, 20 (LXX) is the older Hellenised form. Both forms of spelling occur in P. Lond. 334, 14, 31 (A.D. 166).

531, 14
(2/A.D.)   φαινόλιον, " cloak."

" The transposition of -λ and -ν is common in this word " (G.H.). Cf. the N.T. φελόνης (φαιλόνης), from the Latin ' pænula ' (2 Tim. iv. 13). Cf. O.P. 933 ; 936, 18 (φαινόλιν). In the last instance it may be noted that -ιον becomes -ιν in vulgar Greek. Cf. συνέδριν for συνέδριον, παιδίν for παιδίον.

ἄρσενον, " a male."

The question of form (ἄρρην or ἄρσην) emerges. W.H. read ἄρσην throughout the N.T. ἄρσην is found in P. Gen. 35, 6 (2/A.D.), and ἀρσενικός in Ostra. 1601 ; O.P. 886, 15 ; 38, 7 ; 1216, 14. ἄρρην, which is the latter Attic form, occurs in C.P.R. 28, 12 (A.D. 110) ; B.G.U. 88, 6 (A.D. 147). O.P. 37, 1, 7 has ἀρρενικόν; which is also found in Attic inscriptions. In the LXX ἄρσην is the regular form, but ἄρρην is found in Sir. 36, 26 ; 4 Macc. xv. 30. WITKOWSKI (E.P.G.; p. 132) styles ἄρσενον " forma barbara." It is clear that there was a distinct wavering between ρρ and ρσ. Cf. θάρσει (Matt. ix. 2) and θαρροῦντες (2 Cor. v. 6), θαρροῦντας (Heb. xiii. 6). Cf. MOULTON (Gram., vol. ii. p. 103 f.).

CHAPTER V

EPISTOLARY CHARACTER AND FORM

LETTERS in the papyri contemporary with Christianity assume an added significance when we
reflect upon three facts : (*a*) that the literature
of the N.T. begins historically with private correspondence, namely, that of Paul ; (*b*) that of the
twenty-seven books included in the N.T. canon
twenty-one take the form of epistles ; (*c*) that
epistolary writings form a striking differentia of
the N.T. among sacred books. There is, therefore,
large intrinsic probability that the N.T. has much
to gain from an increasing knowledge of the letters
of the ancient world. The purpose of this chapter
is to discover what light is cast by the Oxyrhynchan
private correspondence upon the epistolary features
of the N.T. The two main questions which
emerge concern (1) the nature of the N.T. epistles
and their distribution between the categories of
' letter ' and ' epistle ' ; (2) their epistolary
form and phraseology. It is not unreasonable to
expect that, from the placing of the N.T. epistles
even in the limited context which these contemporary letters provide, light should fall upon both
these aspects of N.T. study.

A. THE NATURE OF THE N.T. EPISTLES

We have accepted in the main the validity of DEISSMANN'S distinction between ' letter ' and ' epistle.' It may be convenient briefly to recall the essential points. A letter is necessarily personal and self-revealing. Its reality rests upon the intimacy existing between writer and reader. An epistle, on the other hand, tends to become impersonal. This is specially visible in the case of the ' Catholic ' Epistles of the N.T. In an epistle the personal element, whilst not eliminated, is subordinated to some more general and widespread interest. A letter is private, designed for the eye of its addressee ; an epistle aims avowedly at publicity. The wider the constituency of the latter, the more faithfully is its purpose achieved. A letter is unstudied, the spontaneous expression of personal feeling ; an epistle is consciously literary, a work of art.

How, then, does it stand with the N.T. epistles when subjected to these crucial tests ? Are they ' letters ' or ' epistles,' or do they, as ROBERTSON [1] suggests, fall wholly in neither one category nor the other, but constitute one of their own ? We confine the discussion at this point to the Pauline writings, the most voluminous as they are, in many respects, the most valuable of the N.T. epistles. The following considerations may be submitted :—

1. *In the Pauline Epistles the personal element*

[1] *Grammar*, p. 85, note.

7

is the primary factor. Their *raison d'être* is grounded in the Apostle's knowledge of his readers, their needs—and idiosyncrasies—and the problems in part created and in part occasioned by their heathen environment. It is not an exaggeration to say that all his writings are marked, in varying degree of course, by the spontaneous and personal characteristics of ' private letters.' Even in the two cases where Paul had no direct personal relationship with the church he is addressing, that is, Romans (written to a Christian community he had not visited) and Colossians (missioned by his co-worker Epaphras), the note of intimacy finds place (cf. Rom. i. 7–16 ; Col. iv. 7–18). Nearly all (again in differing degree) were evoked by some more or less definite occasion. As he writes Paul is usually under the pressure of a precise situation, e.g. the imminence of some particular peril either of moral declension or of heretical apostasy. Not being able to be present in person,[1] the Apostle communicates his opinion upon various problems of moral behaviour and discipline that disturb the Christian fellowship of the Churches, or warns against some incipient heresy that threatens to undermine the foundation of their faith. Further, the letters are to a high degree a self-revelation of their author. So much so that DEISSMANN [2] is led to remark that " their writer is probably the best-known man of the early Empire ; not one of his celebrated contemporaries has left us such frank confessions." In 2 Cor.,

---

[1] At best, a letter is but a poor substitute for personal conversation (cf. 2 John 12).
[2] *L.A.E.*, p. 290.

for example, Paul lays bare his heart (cf. especially chaps. ii. and xi.). The Philippian Epistle is rich in its disclosure of the humanness of the Apostle. In this aspect, that of their strong personal and self-revealing character, Paul's writings are unmistakably true letters.

2. *On the other hand, features abound which mark a divergence from the mere ordinary letter.* In the first place, Paul's writings have manifestly a higher aim than the interchange of personal news and sentiments. Their subject-matter is lofty. It moves in the realm of great ideas and conceptions. Beneath the emphasis Paul places upon particular aspects of the definite situation which he has in mind lies a deposit of eternal principle. Each local circumstance is viewed against the background of fundamental truth. The doctrinal and didactic, the hortatory and admonitory—all are intermingled in the letters of the Apostle. It could scarcely be otherwise. For Paul wrote not as a mere friend, but as a spiritual father of "children in the gospel" (cf. 1 Thess. ii. 7–8; 1 Cor. iv. 14). To his flock he must be "guide, philosopher and friend." As Christ's apostle his word has the ring of authority—an authority that rests ultimately upon no external commission, but is rooted in his own soul's definite experience of God (cf. Gal. i. 11–12 ff.; 2 Cor. iv. 6). The personal element is intertwined with the homiletic in his messages. As A. H. McNEILE [1] points out, the Apostle's letters were spiritual missives designed for public reading, and represent Paul's ripe Christian experience put at the disposal of his

[1] *St. Paul*, p. 121.

churches. Moreover, the letters of Paul were obviously intended for publicity by transmission [1]— the publicity of the particular church or group of churches to which they are addressed, but publicity none the less. Even in that charming letter which on the face of it is a mere personal or private note, Philemon, the prospect of a wider circle is not absent from view. It is addressed to " Philemon . . . *and to the church in thy house* " (vv. 1–2). In Romans and the encyclical Ephesians the constituency is greatly enlarged. The range of circulation of the Pauline Epistles was necessarily restricted by the relatively few communities for which they had interest and value, but at its lowest it was wider than that of the ordinary letter which rarely found an audience outside the confines of a particular house or family. O.P. 1349 is of interest in this connection. The writer asks the recipient to copy the letter for his mother. COBERN [2] remarks : " The private letters such as those Paul wrote would in that era not only be read by the persons receiving them, but would also naturally be copied and sent to other bands of believers, if only they were thought to contain anything of special interest." There is an explicit reference to this practice in Col. iv. 16. Nor must the careful traces of preparation which research in the Pauline letters reveals be ignored. It is true that for Paul the emphasis lay not upon the form but upon the message it conveyed.

[1] The copying out of Paul's letters exposed them, to some extent, to the possibility of error. Parts of them might be displaced, e.g. Rom. xvi (?).

[2] *New Archæological Discoveries,* pp. 589–590.

But that is not to say that he was insensitive to literary grace or contemptuous of the propriety of fitting lofty thought with noble speech. DEISS-MANN [1] seems to make too much of the supposed unliterary character of Paul's writings. To admit that the swift movement of the Apostle's thought and the urge of his deep feeling burst now and again the narrow bounds of ordered language is not to affirm that his letters were unpremeditated and spontaneous effusions of his pen. Literary art is not absent from the Pauline letters. Rom. viii. 31 ff. and 1 Cor. xiii; xv. 51 f. can surely claim to rank as literature. In those passages—and they do not stand alone—a rare beauty and profundity of thought is wedded to graceful speech.[2]

3. *We may sum up thus.* Paul's writings may be classed as 'letters' in view of the personal element, of the subordination of literary artifice to the emotional pressure of a living theme, of the irregularities of style and grammar due to conversational freedom, and of the fact that they were elicited by some definite exigency known to the Apostle and are characterised by incidental allusions. They may be viewed as 'epistles' in virtue of their exalted message and edificatory aim, their accent of spiritual authority, their appeal to a Christian community rather than to an individual, and in the logical presentation of their case (cf. especially Romans). At the same time the scales are weighted on the side of the 'letter.' Paul's writings are not treatises or

[1] *L.A.E.*, pp. 233–234.
[2] *Vide infra*, p. 163 ff.

homilies furnished with personal headings and epistolary form in order to lend a fictitious vividness and freshness to their appeal. Cf. the *Epistulæ Morales* of SENECA in this respect. They are rather to be regarded as a specific type of 'letters' differentiated in the main from the ephemeral private correspondence of Paul's age by the loftiness of their subject-matter and their intrinsic religious worth. But their essential character as 'letters' must not be lost to sight. As Dr. GLOVER [1] says, "the letters are genuine letters—written for the occasion to particular people, and not meant for us. The stamp of genuineness is on them—of life, real life." They can only be adequately interpreted as they are read first of all as letters, read, that is, in vital relation with their writer and original readers.

Two further matters call for brief treatment at this point.

4. *The historical precedents of the religious letter.* Was Paul's use of the letter for religious purposes an innovation, or an adaptation of existing practice? Dr. MOFFATT [2] points out that the literature of a new religious movement is partly original and partly derivative. It will adopt but also adapt forms and materials that lie to hand. The letter or epistle was already a common literary form in the Jewish and pagan world. A species of philosophic treatise in epistolary form was also not unknown (cf. the epistles of EPICURUS). Among precedents for the use of religious letters

[1] *The Jesus of History*, p. 8.
[2] Art. *The Development of N.T. Literature* in Dr. PEAKE'S *Comm. on the Bible*, p. 602.

before the time of Paul may be mentioned the letter in Jer. xxix. (O.T.), the Epistles of Jeremiah and Baruch (Apocrypha), the letters in 2 Macc. i. 1, 10, and Acts xv. 22, 23 (cf. Acts ix. 2 ; xxii. 5 ; xxviii. 21). It is not easy to ascertain how far synagogal correspondence for religious purposes had become an established habit in Judaism. The letter contained in Acts xv. 22 f. conveyed an important decision of the Jerusalem Council respecting intercommunion with the Gentile Churches. The strict observance of the fourfold prohibition (v. 20) was a necessary condition of fellowship between Jewish Christian and proselyte.

But it may be laid to the credit of Paul that he was the first to give an extensive vogue to the letter as a means of religious instruction (unless the view of some scholars, e.g. J. B. MAYOR, is accepted that the Epistle of James is of pre-Pauline date). Professor BARTLET [1] makes the interesting conjecture that it was by writing letters that Paul came to feel an epistle a fit medium of exposition. It may well be that Paul set the fashion for other N.T. writers of epistles. The Apostle utilised and adapted a current literary model which had only been partially developed. But in appropriating an existing literary device he advanced upon it, especially by infusing into it the warmth, freshness and spontaneity of a private letter. This fact is more apparent, as one would naturally expect, in those letters to Churches (e.g. Philippians) where the bond between apostle and people was intimate and strong. As

[1] Art. *Epistle* in HASTINGS' *Dict. of Bible*, vol. i. p. 730, col. a.

Renan [1] puts it, "l'épître fut ainsi la forme de la littérature chrétienne primitive, forme admirable, parfaitement appropriée a l'état du temps et aux aptitudes naturelles de Paul."

Finally, we must consider briefly :

5. *The use of dictation and shorthand in ancient letter-writing.* The Egyptian papyri make it clear that dictation to a scribe was a well-established custom in the Græco-Roman world. It is on all counts most probable that Paul and other N.T. writers used this method. They did so, not indeed because they were ἀγράμματοι—though the wide employment of amanuenses at that period is probably best explained by the general prevalence of illiteracy among the common people (cf. the frequency in papyrus-letters of the phrase μὴ ἰδιότος γράμματα, "unacquainted with letters ") (cf. Acts iv. 13)—but probably because they could write only slowly or with difficulty (cf. Gal. vi. 11). In 1 Peter v. 12 Silvanus may well have been scribe as well as bearer. Rom. xvi. 22 makes reference to Tertius as Paul's amanuensis. Sosthenes (1 Cor. i. 1) and Timothy not improbably acted in a similar capacity. 2 Thess. iii. 17 ; 1 Cor. xvi. 21 ; Col. iv. 18 show that Paul's usual method was to dictate his letters and to add at the end his authenticating signature. These autographic conclusions find plentiful illustration in the papyri private correspondence, where a signature in a handwriting different from that in the body of the letter is often appended. Cf. O.P. 246, 275, 479.

Questions arise, however, as to the significance

[1] *St. Paul*, p. 230.

of the dictation method for our understanding of the letters thus produced. (*a*) In the first place; did Paul dictate the *verba ipsissima* of his letters ? If so, the scribe would presumably take them down in shorthand and afterwards write them out in full. Or was the Apostle content to give the general sense or substance of his message orally, leaving the scribe to shape and phrase it in words of his own ? Was it Paul's habit to prepare a rough draft of the letter and hand it over for amplification and correction ? Did he exercise any right of personal revision of the letter when penned ? To these questions no certain answer can be given. Probably Paul's method varied according to his own immediate circumstances, the gravity of the theme, and the reliability of his secretary. There is no reason to suppose that any inflexible rule was invariably followed. In some cases, perhaps the majority, Paul would no doubt dictate word for word and his amanuensis would then make a fair copy from the shorthand script. In others, the Apostle would probably convey the general purport of the letter to his scribe, and dictate merely those passages of special importance where verbal exactitude was requisite. Be that as it may, the fact that Paul added frequently autograph sentences and signature suggests that his habit was carefully to revise the secretarial work, and, in view of the fact that forged epistles were not unknown (cf. 2 Thess. ii. 2), to seal it with his own apostolic authority.

(*b*) A further feature of the Pauline correspondence must not be overlooked, namely, that in parts it is an answer to letters received. We may picture Paul, when dictating his reply, holding in his hand a copy of the letter sent by his correspondent. He would take up seriatim the points there set forth, and formulate his answer accordingly. Actual quotation, therefore, from previous correspondence may appear in Paul's letters. MILLIGAN [1] sees in such phrases as " being crafty, I caught you with guile " (2 Cor. xii. 16) taunts hurled against Paul by Jewish Christians. None of these letters addressed to the Apostle has been preserved, but J. RENDEL HARRIS [2] has made an ingenious attempt to reconstruct the original letter to which, as he surmises, 1 Thess. was the answer. He shows that the method is capable of fruitful application to other Pauline Epistles, e.g. 2 Cor. H. A. A. KENNEDY [3] applies it to the case of Philippians; and finds in i. 12, ii. 19, iv. 10, etc., allusions to a letter previously received.

(c) Paul's method of dictation throws light upon certain linguistic and literary features of his letters. Their speech-character, for example, becomes clear. As Paul spoke he would visualise his audience. Hence the letters are marked by a conversational freedom. Grammatical looseness of structure, occasional solecisms and anacoluthia (cf. Rom. v. 12 ; Gal. ii. 5) are thereby explicable. Thought would move too fast for speech. Words would take wing under the pressure of deep emotion. Language would break down " in such high hour of visitation from the living God."

[1] *N.T. Documents*, p. 29.
[2] *Expositor*, vol. viii. p. 161 ff.
[3] *Philippians* (Exp. Gr. Test., p. 403).

The Second Corinthian Epistle in particular is charged with a high voltage of spiritual thought and feeling. A sudden change of tone might be accounted for by interruption and resumption of the dictation process. Further, may not the long sentences and involved periods of, say, Ephesians be due to the fact that the scribe was not expert enough to keep pace with the Apostle's torrential speech ? This is not to charge Paul's coadjutors with incompetence ; nor is it to suggest that the letters were penned without care. That is unthinkable in face of their encyclical character and vital content. Sir F. G. KENYON [1] has reminded us that the Pauline scribes are not to be regarded as " trained professional scribes." Some would naturally be more skilled than others, and this fact is not without significance for differences of style in the letters of Paul.

In line with the use of dictation the art of shorthand was widely diffused. SANDAY and HEADLAM [2] state on the authority of EUSEBIUS that ORIGEN's lectures were taken down in that way. Shorthand was used by literary men, e.g. CICERO and GALEN. In O.P. 724 (A.D. 155) a certain master apprentices his slave to Apollonius, a shorthand writer, for a two years' course of tuition at an agreed charge of one hundred and twenty silver drachmæ. The question emerges in connection with the Pauline speeches incorporated in Acts. How far are they the record of the actual words of the speaker ? CHASE [3] argues for

[1] *Handbook to Text.*, Crit., p. 26.
[2] *Romans*, p. lx (Inter. Crit. Comm.).
[3] *Credibility of Acts*, p. 111 f.

what is now a generally conceded position, viz. that the record in Acts is a substantially accurate report of what Paul said, but the diction, being hardly distinguishable from the narrative portions, is that of Luke. He posits two determining factors : (*a*) editorial latitude ; (*b*) transmission. It is in connection with the latter process that the question of the part played by shorthand arises. At some of Paul's orations Luke was almost certainly present in person, e.g. that to the Ephesian elders. CHASE [1] (taking the speech of Tertullus in Acts xxiv. 2 ff. as a basis for his argument) suggests that Luke took down brief and disjointed shorthand notes which he afterwards worked up and elaborated into the form in which they appear in Acts. The acute conjecture is made that Luke learned shorthand during the course of his medical training. CHASE [2] thinks the speech at Miletus was preserved in the same way, that is, short notes were jotted down and then transcribed and amplified. " It is probable that in the case of the speeches contained in the closing chapters of the Acts, we have, more or less edited and elaborated, a transcript of notes taken, it may well be by St. Luke himself." CHASE'S theory, as he points out,[3] applies only to those speeches which were deliberately prepared for solemn occasions. (Most of the speeches recorded in Acts were largely unpremeditated, being called forth by the exigencies of the moment.)   MOFFATT [4] says : " Of the later

[1] *Credibility of Acts*, p. 111 f.
[2] *Op. cit.*
[3] *Op. cit.*, p. 113 f.
[4] *Introd. to the Literature of the N.T.*, p. 306.

speeches, that at Miletus is probably nearest to a summary of the original words of Paul ; the others, for the most part, reflect in the main Luke's historic sense of what was appropriate to the speaker and situation.   Stephen's speech is the most notable exception ; it obviously was derived from a special source." The historian would take pains, surely, to avoid shaping his materials so freely as to conceal their distinctive aim and tone. PAGE,[1] by detailing words and phrases characteristically Pauline in the speech to the elders of Ephesus (Acts xx. 18-35), shows that the plea of editorial manipulation should not be unduly pressed.   McLACHLAN has a full discussion of the question in his *St. Luke, the Man and His Work*, p. 175 f.

B. BRIEF CHARACTERISATION OF THE LITERARY FORM OF THE N.T. EPISTLES.

1. The Pauline Epistles.

These comprise (following the approximate chronological order outlined by FINDLAY [2]) 1 and 2 Thess., 1 and 2 Cor., Gal., Rom., Col., Philem., Eph. (assuming the Pauline authorship of the last named, which some scholars reject), and Philippians.   DEISSMANN [3] does not hesitate to classify all these writings under the heading of 'real letters.'   The dominant personal element, together with intimate knowledge of the readers and their

[1] *Acts of the Apostles*, p. xxxvi.
[2] *Epistles of Paul the Apostle*, p. 25 f.
[3] Art. *Epistolary Literature*, in *Encyc. Bib.*, col. 1327.

needs, which we have seen to be the outstanding features of a genuine letter, lends force to his view. But the statement calls for qualification. More allowance should be made for the varying degree of conformity to the standard of a true letter which the Pauline correspondence reveals. It must be more frankly admitted that confidence in assigning a particular book to the category of ' letter ' or ' epistle ' is not always well grounded. The border line in not a few cases is obviously thin. For example, there can be no question that Philemon is a private and personal letter, thoroughly human and self-revealing. But at the other end of the scale stands the weighty Epistle to the Romans which in its general tenor and form is a far remove from the unstudied private note, and suggests to some an open letter addressed to a church and to others an ordered treatise set forth in epistolary mode. (Rom. xvi., which may be a separate letter, must be excepted. It abounds in personal greetings and keeps close to the pattern of a true ' letter.') The case is similar, though in less degree, with Ephesians, which is presumably of an encyclical character. Moreover, the congregational outlook, speech-character and didactic tone of the Thessalonian, Corinthian and Colossian Epistles are elements which cannot be left out of account, though 2 Cor. shows many features of a true ' letter.'

2. The Pastoral Epistles.

1 and 2 Tim. and Titus may be classified in the main as ' letters.' They are a combination

of private notes and pseudepigraphy, and not improbably embody portions derived from genuine letters of Paul.

3. The General Epistles.

1 and 2 Peter conform to the general type of " epistle." Jude and James (the latter has a formal address but no concluding greeting) suggest homilies in epistolary form. DEISSMANN [1] says " that they cannot be real letters is evident from the outset by their addresses ; a letter to the ' twelve tribes scattered abroad ' could not be forwarded as a letter." 1 John is a religious manifesto ; 2 John a note to some individual Christian or to a Church which is personified under the figure of ἐκλεκτὴ κυρία (" the elect lady "). 3 John is distinctly a real letter, being a private communication addressed to a friend.

4. The Epistle to the Hebrews.

This book suggests written notes of discourses. " Hebrews is, like James, a homily in epistolary form." So MOFFATT.[2] It belongs, therefore, to the category of ' epistles.' Its author and audience are alike obscure.

5. Two letters in Acts.

(a) xv. 23–29. A synodical epistle.
(b) xxiii. 26–30. Largely of the nature of a private note sent to a superior (Felix).

[1] Art. *Epistolary Literature*, col. 1328.
[2] *Introd. to the Literature of the N.T.*, p. 428.

It may be noted that the insertion of letters in historical documents was a common usage of Græco-Roman times. So DEISSMANN.[1] Cf. 2 Macc. i. 1, 10.

6. The letters to the Seven Churches in the Apocalypse.

These are pastoral letters replete with local allusions and admonitions to the Churches. There is no evidence that they ever enjoyed circulation apart from the apocalyptic book in which they appear. They form probably a series of prophetic addresses couched in epistolary form, and accordingly fall into the class of 'epistles.' RAMSAY [2] objects that DEISSMANN'S division into 'letters' and 'epistles' is too rigid and narrow. The letters to the Seven Churches he places in a new category, viz. that of "a general letter addressed to a whole congregation or to the entire Church of Christ."

C. EPISTOLARY FORM AND PHRASEOLOGY.

It is the aim of this section to show the similarity between the letters of the N.T. and contemporary private correspondence as regards (1) their structure and order, (2) the use of stereotyped epistolary phrases and formulæ found markedly in the more formal parts of a letter.

[1] *B.S.*, p. 28, note 5.
[2] *Letters to the Seven Churches*, p. 23 f.

1. Order and structure.

A casual review of the private correspondence in the papyri reveals the fact that the letters of the period followed a regular and established order and were shaped in a well-defined way. Variations in both sequence and structure are, of course, apparent, but in the main the skeletal form of a papyrus letter is easily discerned. As a rule, the customary epistolary formulæ turn on the following : (a) thanksgiving for good news and expression of good wishes ; (b) prayers for welfare of body and soul and also for worldly prosperity. The order of procedure may be sketched somewhat as follows :—

Opening address or salutations.
Thanksgiving and prayer for addressee.
The substance of the letter containing directions and personal news, etc.
Farewell greetings and closing prayer.

A perusal of the Pauline letters in particular shows clearly their affinity with this outline of epistolary structure. The needs of readers and the exigencies of local circumstances necessitated an occasional variation in order and emphasis, but the Apostle followed in the main the regular epistolary plan, inserting, as was his wont, before closing salutations and benediction, exhortation and ethical teaching. The Epistle to the Philippians may be taken as a typical example. An analysis of the letter reveals its epistolary framework thus :—

i. 1-3. Opening address and greeting.
i. 3-11. Thanks to God for Paul's remem-
8

brance of his Philippian converts, and prayers on their behalf.

i. 12–iv. 20. The substance of the letter consisting of :

    (*a*) personal news and disclosure of deep feeling ;

    (*b*) exposition of the manner of life worthy of the Gospel, the mind of Christ, joy in the Lord, and a parenthesis *re* Timothy and Epaphroditus ;

    (*c*) exhortation, counsels of reconciliation and acknowledgment of the Philippian generosity.

iv. 21–22. Closing salutations.

iv. 23. Benediction.

We may sum up in the words of FINDLAY (*Epp. to Thess.* in *Camb. Gr. Test.*, p. lxi) : " The general form of the letters of St. Paul is moulded on the epistolary style of the period ; and this is specially evident in their commencement and conclusion."

2. Epistolary phrases and formulæ.

(*a*) *Salutations.*

The generous proportion of personal greetings in a private letter is quite in keeping with its essential character as a fresh and intimate communication between absent friends. The habit of the letter writer is to open with a brief general salutation, longer and particularised greetings being reserved, as a rule, for the end of the letter. This, however, is by no means an invariable method. There are cases, e.g. O.P. 525, where the opening salutation is lacking. In this respect 1 John and Hebrews may be noticed. (See MOFFATT'S *Introd. to the Literature of the N.T.*, pp. 428–429, for the bearing of this point on the literary character of the Epistle to the Hebrews.) The abrupt beginning in both is quite consistent with the relative subordination of the personal element, one being of the nature of a pastoral manifesto, the other of a treatise. Again, by way of exception, in O.P. 298 the writer's greetings appear in the middle (not at the end) of his note, and in O.P. 295 and 525 (referred to above) there is an entire absence of merely personal expressions in the whole letter. But a list of personal greetings closing the communication is a markedly common feature in papyri private correspondence. MILLIGAN (*Select.*, p. xxvi, note) cites B.G.U. 601 (2/A.D.) as a case in point. It is to be noted that the same feature appears in the Pauline letters, e.g. Rom. xvi. 3 f., Col. iv. 10 f. Paul allots a generous portion of his space to the conveyance of greetings from his co-workers and himself, the two epistles mentioned above being specially rich in personal salutations.

The following examples of epistolary greetings may be noted from the private correspondence found at Oxyrhynchus.

εὐψυχεῖν.

O.P.

115, 2
(2/A.D.)

" Good cheer." Paul's use of the word in Phil. ii. 19 may be coloured by its epistolary significance. It occurs here in a letter of condolence and was

O.P.   common in epitaphs. It is not found in classical
Greek, but occurs in Josephus, *Antiq.* xi. vi. 9.

292, 2   χαίρειν, " greeting."
(A.D. 25)

A common Greek formula of a greeting found
at the beginning of a letter, corresponding to the
Eastern ' peace ' (שָׁלֹם).   Cf. Ezra iv. 17 ; Acts
xv. 23 (letter of the apostles and elders) ; Acts
xxiii. 26 (letter of Claudius Lysias to Felix) ;
Jas. i. 1.   Cf. 2 John 10, 11 ; Luke x. 6.

Grammatically, χαίρειν is the absolute use of
the infinitive, and there appears to be no need to
posit ellipsis of a verb of command, as BLASS
supposed (*Gram.*, p. 222).   The imperative χαίρε
is sometimes used.   Cf. O.P. 112 (χαίροις), 122,
1482, 1664, 1667 (χαίρε).   In 2 Macc. i. 10 and
ix. 19 we find the phrase χαίρειν καὶ ὑγιαίνειν,
" greeting and health."

293, 16   ἐπισκοποῦ δὲ ὑμᾶς καὶ πάντας τοὺς ἐν οἴκῳ, " take
(A.D. 27)   care of yourself and all at home."

The name of an individual is often followed by
a phrase including his household.   Cf. 2 Tim. iv. 19.
Cf. also Rom. xvi. 5, τὴν κατ' οἶκον αὐτῶν ἐκκλησίαν
(" the church that is in their house ") and especially Phil. iv. 22 with the common epistolary
refrain " all who are here salute you."   Cf. O.P.
743, 43 ἐπισκοποῦ τοὺς σοὺς πάντες (" look after all
your household "), and O.P. 294, 31 ; Heb. xii. 15
(ἐπισκοποῦντες).

300, 9   ἀσπάζομαι, " I salute (you)."
(late
1/A.D.)   " So and so salutes you " (ἀσπάζεται σε) is
common in both papyri and N.T.   It is usually

a concluding greeting. J. ARM. ROBINSON (*Comm. on Eph.*, p. 280) shows that three forms of the greeting were in common vogue, (*a*) ἀσπάζομαι, (*b*) ἀσπάσαι, (*c*) ἀσπάζεται. The use of the first person ἀσπάζομαι in Rom. xvi. 22 is illustrated by O.P. 1067, 25 (3/A.D.). προσαγορεύω (" I address ") was apparently a variant in use. It occurs alone in O.P. 526, 2 ; 928, 14 ; 1664, 2, and in combination with ἀσπάζομαι in 1070, 47. It occurs in the N.T only once (Heb. v. 10), in the participial form.

εὐτύχει, " farewell."

526, 13
(2/A.D.)

Regularly used to conclude a letter addressed to an adult or superior. εὐτύχει is not found in the N.T. εὐτυχία occurs in O.P. 1766, 12, and εὐτυχεῖν in O.P. 396 ; 805.

ἔρρωσο (ἔρρωσθε), " farewell."

530, 29
(2/A.D.)

ἔρρωσθε is found once in the N.T. (Acts xv. 29). ἔρρωσο in Acts xxiii. 30 is presumably a later addition (so W.H.). Apart from MSS. attestation, a point that tells incidentally against the genuineness of ἔρρωσο in Acts xxiii. 30 is that the word is more usual in letters addressed to an equal or inferior. This is confirmed in the main by Egyptian papyri usage (cf. F. G. KENYON in *H.D.B.*, vol. v. p. 356, col. 1). Acts xxiii. 26 f. is a letter written by the military tribune (Claudius Lysias) to the procurator (Felix).

κατ᾿ ὄνομα.

533, 28
(2/3/A.D.)

" Individually," " one by one." Frequently used at the end of a letter where several names are

O.P. mentioned in a greeting. Cf. 3 John 14 ; O.P.
123, 23 ; 298, 34 ; 523, 27 ff. ; 1070, 46 (*passim*).
It is not found in Paul's letters.

(*b*) *Titles and forms of address.*

744, 2
(B.C. 1) Βεροῦτι τῇ κυρίᾳ μου.

"To Berous my lady." This courteous mode
of address may illustrate 2 John i. 5. The usual
identification of κυρία in that passage as either
(*a*) " the church " or (*b*) " a lady of distinction " is
probably to be surrendered in favour of this
epistolary significance "dear friend." Cf. O.P.
886, 1 (3/A.D.), Μεγάλη Ἶσις ἡ κυρία, " Great is the
Lady Isis." ROBERTSON (*Gram.*, p. 173), following
HATCH, states that " κυρία is a common proper
name." Cf. O.P. 1679, 15–17, ὥστε, κυρία, μὴ
μετεωρίζου, " So, lady, do not be anxious."

The use of κύριος as a polite form of address calls
for notice. It is found frequently in reference to
the Roman Emperor (especially Nero). Cf. O.P.
110, 2 ; 1068, 1, 2 ; Acts xxv. 26. Similarly,
κυριακός is common in the papyri in the sense of
" imperial." (See *L.A.E.*, p. 263 f., 353 f.) JÜLICHER
is thus shown to be mistaken in affirming that
Paul invented the term. As H. A. A. KENNEDY
(*Theology of the Epistles*, p. 83) says " The peoples
of the Hellenistic epoch were familiar with the
Divine significance of κύριος. It was a typically
Oriental title. It was constantly used of characteristically Oriental deities, such as the Egyptian
Isis, Osiris, and Serapis. In the first century it
was quickly taking its place as the designation
of the deified Emperor, and thus becoming the

central term of the Imperial cult." What Paul
did, therefore, was to adopt this current title,
and invest it with a deeper and more spiritual
meaning. Its application to earthly emperors was
to him abhorrent. See, for example, his language
in Phil. ii. 11 ; 1 Cor. viii. 5 f. Cf. DEISSMANN'S
B.S., p. 83 f. ROBERTSON (*Gram.*, p. 116) well says
" The Christians did not shrink from using these
words in spite of the debased idea due to the
emperor-cult, Mithraism, or other popular super-
stitions." (It may be observed in passing that
the term " Son of God " (Matt. xxvii. 54) was
regularly ascribed to the Cæsars. Cf. an early
inscription of Augustus found at Tarsus.) This
title belonged of right to their " Lord " (cf. Jude 4).
Its ascription to the deified Roman ruler was
anathema. There was but " one Lord, Jesus
Christ " (1 Cor. viii. 6). To the writers of the
N.T. the risen Christ is, above all else, " Lord "
(cf. Phil. ii. 9–11).

COBERN (*New Archæological Discoveries*, p. 127)
points out that the application of the term Κύριος
to Jesus seems to have been a distinct ascription
of deity to Christ, since the title Κύριος could be
used only after the Cæsar had been acknowledged
as God. It is, therefore, an incidental piece of
evidence in determining the view held by the
early Church concerning Christ. How soon the
worship of Jesus as " Lord " began is a moot
question of N.T. scholarship. In view of the
fact that the term Κύριος was a common LXX
rendering of a Divine name there is nothing
improbable in the belief that the early followers
of Jesus transferred to him a title which seemed

O.P. adequately to fit their high estimate of his
person.[1]

DALMAN (*Words of Jesus*, p. 324 ff.) has a section
on " ' The Lord,' as a designation of Jesus."

1486, 1   Under this section we may note Ξενικὸς [ὁ] καὶ
(3/4/A.D). Πέλιος " Xenicus also called Pelius " in O.P. 1486.
The phrase is an exact parallel to Acts xiii. 9,
Σαῦλος δέ, ὁ καὶ Παῦλος (" Saul, who is also *called*
Paul "). Egyptian census-lists contain many such
double names, suggesting that it was customary
for the inhabitants to assume a Greek or Roman
name in addition to their own. It is improbable,
therefore, that Saul adopted the name Paul from
his eminent convert Sergius Paulus (Acts xiii. 7).
It is more likely that he bore the double name
all along, but discontinued the use of his Jewish
name when he entered upon his Gentile mission.
DEISSMANN (*B.S.*, p. 313 f.) has an excursus on the
point of double nomenclature. Cf. Acts i. 23 ;
Col. iv. 11.

1680, 20   τῷ κυρίῳ καὶ ἀγαπητῷ πατρὶ Ἀπόλλωνι, " to my
(3/4/A.D.) lord and beloved father, Apollo."

A regular form of address strongly suggesting
Christian sentiments. Cf. Matt. iii. 17. J. ARM.
ROBINSON (*Comm. on Eph.*, p. 229 f.) deals fully
with ἀγαπητός as a Messianic title.

(c) *Prayers and requests.*

μνείαν σου ποιούμενος ἐπὶ τῶν προσευχῶν.

" Making mention of thee in (my) prayers."

[1] Both Hebrew names Yahweh and Adonāi were rendered in the LXX by the term Κύριος. Cf. Psa. cx. 1
(Matt. xxii. 44).

Cf. Rom. i. 9 f.; Eph. i. 16 ; 1 Thess. i. 2 ; Philem.
4 ; 2 Tim. i. 3. This phrase (common in inscriptions) is often qualified by some adverbial expression such as διὰ πάντος, "continually." The use
of this conventional phrase shows clearly Paul's
knowledge of Greek epistolary style. "Like some
other phrases in St. Paul, it is an old expression
of the religious life of the people, lifted up to its
highest use" (J. ARM. ROBINSON's *Comm. on
Eph.*, p. 37). The fuller phrase of 1 Thess. i. 2–3
is probably a development of the above (*op. cit.*,
p. 279).

ἐρρῶσθαι σε εὔχομαι, " I pray that you may be well."
A common epistolary phrase. Cf. 3 John 2. It
occurs usually at the beginning of a letter, but is
found at the end in O.P. 292, 11 ; 931, 10. A
variant is καὶ προκόπτειν εὔχομαι. Cf. O.P. 122, 15 ;
Luke ii. 52. As above, an adverbial expression of
time is often found in conjunction, e.g. πολλοῖς
χρόνοις. Cf. O.P. 1066, 1068, 1157, 1221 *al.* Kindred
phrases are found in O.P. 933, 1216, 1217, 396
(διὰ παντὸς ἐρρωμένῳ εὐτυχεῖν). πρὸ μὲν ποντὸς
εὔχομαι σε ὑγιαίνειν, " before all else I pray that you
may be in health," occurs in O.P. 528, 529, 936,
1158. Dr. RENDEL HARRIS (Art. *A Study in
Letter Writing*, p. 167 in *Expositor*, 1898) makes the
acute suggestion that the περὶ πάντων of 3 John 2
should be emended to πρὸ πάντων to conform to
papyrus letters.

καὶ εὔχομαι τῷ θεῷ ὁλοκληρεῖν σε καὶ εὐοδοῦσθαι.
" I pray God that you may have health and
prosperity." Cf. 3 John 2 for a close parallel.

O.P.   (d) *Commendations and injunctions.*

First we must notice that there are six instances in these papyri of the ἐπιστολὴ συστατική, " letter of recommendation " (O.P. 292, 746, 1162, 1219, 1587, 787). The practice of sending commendatory letters was apparently common and is referred to in the N.T. (Acts ix. 2, xxii. 5 ; 1 Cor. xvi. 3 (R.V.) ; 2 Cor. iii. 1). Cf. Acts xviii. 27, where it is recorded that the brethren wrote to the disciples to receive Paul who was about to pass over into Achaia. The Epistle to Philemon, Rom. xvi. 1–2, 3 John are apparently actual examples in the N.T. of " letters of commendation." The abrupt opening in Rom. xvi. 1 (συνίστημι δὲ) is paralleled in papyrus-letters, e.g. *Epistolographi Græci* (pp. 259, 659). In O.P. 1587 the phrase used is συστατικῶν γραμμάτων. In O.P. 1070, 49 the phrase γράμματα καὶ ἐπιστολαί, " notes and letters," is found. *M.M.* (p. 131) affirm that " when γράμμα becomes collective its primary meaning is ' a letter.' " This meaning would suit the context in O.P. 1587 ; 938, 18, but the collocation of the two terms in 1070, 49 suggests some distinction, however subtle. " But it may be a paper or document of any kind " (*ibid.*). Cf. Luke xvi. 6 (' bond ').

113, 6   εὖ ποιήσεις (οr καλῶς ποιήσεις).
(2/A.D.)

Commonly introduces a command or request, ' please.' Cf. 3 John 6 ; Phil. iv. 14 ; Acts x. 33 ; 2 Peter i. 19. It is usually followed by the aorist participle of coincident action, though occasionally by the infinitive or even indicative, e.g. O.P. 1672, 12. In O.P. 929, 7, 17 the phrase is followed first by an aorist participle (ἀπαιτήσας) and then by the infinitive (ἀποκαταστῆσαι). Cf. O.P. 116, 5; 294, 12; 300, 5 *al.*

εὖ πράσσειν, " good-bye."

Cf. Acts xv. 29. The phrase would seem sometimes to be almost synonymous with ἔρρωσθε, with which it is conjoined in 2 Macc. ix. 19; Acts xv. 29. Cf. O.P. 822 where "it takes the place of χαίρειν" (G.H.). καλῶς ἔπραξας, "you did well," occurs in O.P. 1067, 3 (cf. 1155, 8).

ὁ ἀποδιδούς σοι κ.τ.λ.

"The bearer" (of a letter). Cf. O.P. 746, 3; Luke iv. 20. ἀναδίδωμι in the same sense occurs in 532, 11. Cf. 1063, 14; 1295, 15; 1667, 4; 1757, 12. The simple δίδωμι is found in 937, 30. In O.P. 293, 20 ἀπόδος is used as a formula of transmission, "pass on."

μὴ οὖν ἄλλως ποιήσῃς.

"Be sure you do." Cf. O.P. 745, 8. It is a frequent phrase in letters conveying an urgent request.

ἐρωτῶ δὲ σε καὶ παρακαλῶ, "I beg and beseech you."

Cf. O.P. 744, 6; 1 Thess. iv. 1. For διὸ παρακαλῶ σε in O.P. 292, 5, cf. Acts xxvii. 34; 2 Cor. ii. 8.

σεαυτοῦ ἐπιμέλου εἶν' ὑγιαίνῃς, "take care of yourself that you may be well."

O.P.

Cf. O.P. 743 ; 745 ; 805 ; 1154, 4 ; Luke x. 34 f. ;
1 Tim. iii. 5. The verb takes the dative in O.P.
744, 6 ; 1 Esdras vi. 26. See above, p. 78.

295, 2
(A.D. 35)

γινώσκειν σε θέλω (or γίνωσκε), " I would have you
know."

Very commonly used to open a letter after the
introductory greeting. Cf. O.P. 528 ; 743 ; 937 ;
1155 ; 1481 ; Rom. i. 13 ; 1 Cor. xi. 3 ; Phil. i. 12 ;
Col. ii. 1 ; Heb. xiii. 23. M.M. (p. 127) say " it
will be noticed that the phrase does not come
into regular use till early 2/A.D., which accounts
for the N.T. showing a phrase (οὐ θέλω ὑμᾶς ἀγνοεῖν
in Paul) with the same meaning but with form not
yet crystallised." The N.T. examples show that
the phrase was still fluid in form.

1293, 7
(A.D.
117–138)

δήλωσόν μοι.

" Let me know." Cf. O.P. 1294, 16 ; 1488, 7 ;
1495, 9. Δηλόω is very common.

1663, 8
(2/3/A.D.)

παρατίθεμαί σοι . . . Σερῆνον, " I commend to
thee, Serenus. Cf. Acts xiv. 23 ; xx. 32.

(e) Miscellaneous.

It remains now to set down a few epistolary
phrases which do not fall into any distinctive
category.

113, 13
(2/A.D.)

χάρις τοῖς θεοῖς (or χάριν ἔχω θεοῖς), "thanks be to
the gods."

A phrase expressing satisfaction or thanks.
The common χάρις δὲ τῷ Θεῷ in the Pauline
Epistles (Rom. vi. 17 ; vii. 25 R.V.m. ; and cf

2 Tim. i. 3 ; 1 Tim. i. 12 for a variant of the phrase) suggests an adaptation by Paul in the direction of a staunch monotheism of what was virtually a polytheistic formula in the current language. So here, χάριν ἔχω θεοῖς is analogous to χάριν ἔχω τῷ Θεῷ in 2 Tim. i. 3. J. ARM. ROBINSON (*Comm. on Eph.*, p. 224 f.) argues that the use of χάρις in the Pauline Epistles is a sort of sign-manual of the Apostle authenticating, as it were, his epistles. Cf. 2 Thess. iii. 17–18.

ἐχάρην (λίαν ἐχάρην), " I rejoiced (greatly)."
    Also expresses satisfaction. Cf. Phil. iv. 10 ; 2 John 4 ; 3 John 3.

τὰ κατ' ἐμε, " my affairs."   120, 14
    Cf. Acts xxiv. 22 ; Rom. i. 15 ; Eph. vi. 21 ; ⁽⁴/A.D.⁾ Col. iv. 7 ; Phil. i. 12 ; Tobit x. 8.

πρὸ μὲν πάντων, " before all else."   294, 30
    Cf. O.P. 292, 11. This phrase occurring at the (A.D. 22) end of a letter illustrates Jas. v. 12.

καλῶς ποιήσεις ἀντιφωνήσασά μοι ὅτι ἐκομίσου.   300, 5
    " Please send me back word that you have (1/A.D.) received it." ἀντιφωνεῖν seems to have a special epistolary flavour, " to give an answer." Cf. 1 Macc. xii. 18 ; O.P. 805, 3. The substantive (" answer ") occurs in O.P. 294, 29. Not in N.T.

    A postscript is a familiar device in letter-writing.   396
If the letter was dictated, the sender would sign (1/A.D.) his name and sometimes add a postscript. Cf. 1 Cor. xvi. 21 ; Col. iv. 18. An example of an autograph

O.P. signature appears in O.P. 1491. In O.P. 1067,
25 (3/A.D.), to a letter written by a certain Helene
to her brother their father adds κἀγὼ 'Αλέξανδρος
ὁ πατὴρ ὑμῶν ἀσπάζομαι ὑμᾶς πολλά (" and I, too,
Alexander your father, send you many greetings "). The example clearly illustrates the postscript by Tertius in Rom. xvi. 22. In O.P. 396 it
is noteworthy that the addendum is placed at
the top of the letter, and not as usually (cf. O.P.
1481) at the foot.

939
(4/A.D.)

A group of these Oxyrhynchan letters seems
distinctively Christian in tone and thought, e.g.
939 ; 1161 ; 1162 ; 1298 ; 1299 ; 1492–1495 ;
1592 ; 1774 (where the writer uses the phrase
αἱ αδελφαὶ ἐν Κυρίῳ), " sisters in the Lord."
See below, p. 147 f. O.P. 939 abounds in N.T.
echoes, e.g. ἐν θλίψει, " in affliction." Cf. 1 Thess. i. 6 ;
Eph. iii. 13. MILLIGAN (*Epp. to the Thess.*, p. 111)
says that θλίψις is " a good example of a word
transformed to meet a special want in the religious
vocabulary." It bears in profane Greek (where
the word is rare) the meaning ' pressure.' In
the N.T. it is used metaphorically, ' affliction.'
O.P. 1682, 6 has the phrase ἡ μὲν τοῦ θεοῦ πρόνοια
παρέξει, " may the Divine Providence grant," etc.,
which suggests Christian influence. DEISSMANN
(*Encyc. Bib.*, col. 3560) calls attention to the fact
that many private letters of otherwise unknown
Christians await the attention of the scholar.

1063
(2/3/A.D.)

Here the writer's name is not given. In O.P.
1162, 14 the writer's signature is attested by a
certain Emmanuel, 'Εμμανουὴλ μάρτυς.

ἀναψύχομεν (" I take relaxation ") here suggests
a note on the usage apparent in many papyrus
letters of an epistolary first person plural. The
question has been raised in regard to the first
person plural found in the Pauline Epistles (e.g.
2 Cor. i. 8–11 ; iv. 7–15). It is probably a safe
rule to interpret it as an editorial ' we,' but only
where the context demands it. In several cases
Paul may be including others with himself. Indeed, this applies also to some of the papyri
instances of the first person plural. The papyri
examples of alternate ἡμεῖς and ἐγώ suggest that
no hard-and-fast rule can be laid down in respect
to Paul's usage of these pronouns. See MILLIGAN'S
reasoned statement (*Epp. to the Thess.*, note B,
p. 131 f.).

O.P.
1296, 7
(3/A.D.)

The fact that some letters contain writing on
the *verso*, that is, the back of the papyrus sheet,
throws light upon Ezek. ii. 9 f., Rev. v. 1 f.
The roll was so full that the contents overflowed
to the back of the sheet, so that it was " written
within and on the back."

CHAPTER VI

SUBJECT-MATTER AND THOUGHT

IT has become axiomatic that no religious movement can be adequately interpreted apart from
its historic setting. The drift of Biblical science
is to place more and more emphasis upon the
contact of Christianity with the age in which it
arose. This does not mean the tacit assumption
that Christianity was a product of its time. Its
roots lie deeper. Christianity is more adequately
explained by its O.T. background than by its
Hellenistic environment.[1] But what that environment fails to account for it may serve to illuminate.
Now the non-literary papyri in general provide
glimpses into the conditions of their era which
are the more lifelike because they are uninten-
tional. It is the aim of this chapter to discover
what light is thrown by these letters in particular
on the historic environment of primitive Christianity, and to mark, especially, any points of
contact or contrast with N.T. thought which may

[1] The term 'Hellenistic environment' signifies roughly
the civilised world contemporary with Christianity, which,
though essentially Greek at heart, embosomed wider racial
and cultural forces.

emerge. It is to be noted that the allusions which have significance for our enquiry are largely of an incidental character. But for that reason they are of greater value. The charm of a true letter often lies less in what it says than in what it unwittingly suggests. It must be read between the lines with sympathy and imagination ; a chance word or fleeting reference may light up for the reader the whole contour of the writer's situation. The present collection of letters is, as we have seen, typical of its kind. Their writers had no idea that they were really laying bare the domestic, social and cultural features of their age. None the less, they have unknowingly rendered that eminent service ; their artless letters have created for posterity a kind of impressionist picture of the historic background of Christian origins. We may therefore confidently approach this mass of correspondence from the point of view of its occasional and incidental allusions. Even the most trivial of these may open a window through which we may view in clearer outline the landscape of early Christian times. The salient points may be classified as follows.

A. Personal and Domestic.

1. In O.P. 119 (2/3/A.D.) we have " a picture of ancient family life." Theon *fils* reproves his father for going off to Alexandria without him, and ironically thanks him for sending " great gifts . . . locust-beans." The letter is full of subtle humour and incidentally reveals the happy

and intimate relationship between father and son. The latter is evidently an *enfant terrible*. His mother cries in distraction " Away with him ! " (line 10). O.P. 939 provides a peep into a happy and united home circle. The servant's tender solicitude for his sick mistress and the comfort he holds out by the hourly expectation of his master's arrival assume an added significance if, as is probable from the internal evidence, the letter shows signs of Christian influence. It recalls Paul's valuation of Onesimus, " more than a servant, a brother beloved " (Philem. 16). The solvent of social disparities lay in the establishment of Christian relationships. Kindness within the family circle is strongly enjoined by Epictetus and Plutarch. Cf. O.P. 1067, where a certain Helene reproves her brother for not attending their brother's funeral. Disloyalty to the obligations of kinship was evidently deeply felt among the ancients. Cf. the sororal affection of Antigone for her brother Polynices and her determination that his corpse shall not lack the honour of ritual burial. It is the unbrotherly attitude of the elder son that gives poignancy to Jesus' homely Parable of the Prodigal Son (Luke xv. 11 ff.).

2. The writer of O.P. 294 (A.D. 22), away from home on legal business, hears that his house has been searched during his absence. He sends to a certain Dorion for information, and says: " I am not so much as anointing myself until I hear word from you on each point " (line 14). Similarly in O.P. 528 (2/A.D.) a husband, putting in a plea that his wife should return to him, says: " Since we

bathed together on Phaophi 12, I never bathed
nor anointed myself until Athur 12 " (line 9 f.),
that is, he abstained for exactly one month.

Both these excerpts throw light on a passage
like Matt. vi. 16–18. A protest against some action
often takes the form of abstinence from food and
drink and other physical necessities. Cf. the above-
mentioned papyrus letter (119) where the schoolboy author threatens neither to eat nor drink
unless his absent father invites him to join in a
tour to Alexandria. DEISSMANN [1] compares with
this voluntary asceticism the resolution of the
Jewish zealots in Acts xxiii. 12, 21.

Among the Jews anointing of the head and face
was a daily toilet practice (cf. Psa. civ. 15), usually
after washing (cf. Ruth iii. 3 ; Ezek. xvi. 9).
Its discontinuance was a sign of mourning (cf.
Dan. x. 2–3) : " In those days I Daniel was mourning three whole weeks. I ate no pleasant bread,
neither came flesh nor wine in my mouth, neither
did I anoint myself at all, till three whole weeks
were fulfilled." [2] Displeasure (on God's part) is
marked by the cessation of anointing among the
people (Deut. xxviii. 40 ; Mic. vi. 15). In the
East generally anointing was regarded as a symbol
of joy and welcome. Cf. the practice of anointing
the head or feet of a guest on arrival ; cf. Psa. xxiii.
5 ; Luke vii. 36–46 ; and Mary's anointing of
Jesus (John xi. 2). Bathing was customary,
especially before appearing in the presence of
superiors (Ruth iii. 3 ; Judith x. 3). Public baths
are met with in the Greek period (1 Macc. i. 14 ;

[1] *L.A.E.*, p. 189, note 6.
[2] Cf. 2 Sam. xii. 20 ; xiv. 2.

2 Macc. iv. 9, 12), and relics of baths used in the
Roman period have been found. "Public baths
with an amazing equipment (sometimes with a
library) are found in every town, however small." [1]
Ablutions became of increasing ceremonial significance among the Jews (cf. Mark vii. 1 f.).

3. In O.P. 1680 (3/4/A.D.) a son is anxious about
his father's prolonged absence. He makes the
striking suggestion that his father should be
branded with some stamp for identification purposes (σῆμα ἠθέλησα ἐνχαράξαι σοι, "I wanted to
stamp a mark on you"). Paul's 'stigmata'
(Gal. vi. 17) come to mind at once. It was customary to brand horses, cattle and runaway
slaves with a mark of permanent ownership.
In the Roman army recruits were branded, after
testing, for military purposes, and cases are not
unknown of worshippers bearing the name of the
deity branded on their bodies as an attestation of
their consecration to his service.[2] In Gal. vi. 17
the thought suggested is probably that of ownership. "Let no one interfere with me after this,
for I bear branded on my body the owner's stamp
of Jesus" (MOFFATT'S trans.). Cf. the mark
(χάραγμα) branded on the forehead or right hand
in Rev. xiii. 16. For another suggested explana-
tion of 'stigmata' as 'protective marks' see
DEISSMANN (*B.S.*, p. 349 ff.).

B. Social and Political.

1. We have seen that no less than sixteen

---

[1] *The Environment of Early Christianity* (ANGUS), p. 14.
[2] So LIGHTFOOT (*Comm. on Gal.*) interprets Gal. vi. 17.

letters in the Oxyrhynchan collection take the
form of invitations to feasts,[1] some being to private
parties (wedding or birthday celebrations), others
to a religious or ceremonial feast " at the table of
the lord Serapis." There are several points of
interest in these notes of invitation. In the majority
the name of the guest is not mentioned (e.g. 110,
111, 523, 747, 926–7). O.P. 1214, where the guest
is named, is an exception. Further, the hour of
dining seems variable. The fashionable time
appears to have been in the early afternoon, about
3 p.m. Cf. ἀπὸ ὥρας θ′ (110, 111, 523, 926–7).
But ἀπὸ ὥρας η = 8 p.m. occurs in 747, 1486–7,
1580, whilst in 1214 and 1485 the hour is 7 o'clock.
Perhaps the variation was due to the change of
time of sunrise, which varies about two hours in
Egypt.[2] MOULTON [3] points out that if the usual
hour (3 p.m.) held good for Palestine also, light
is thrown upon Christ's reference to the marriage
feast (Matt. xxii. 1–14). It begins in the day-
light and ends at night. In the parable the people
invited are represented as going on with the work
of the day, and the king comes in to see his guests
in the evening. The guest who appears without
a wedding garment is thrown into ' the outer
darkness,' that is, it was night before the marriage
feast reached its conclusion.

The main interest of these letters of invitation
lies in their bearing upon the question of the
participation by Christians in heathen feasts.
1 Cor. viii., x. 14 ff., show that the issue was

[1] *Vide supra*, p. 44 f.
[2] So G.H. in O.P., vol. xii. p. 244.
[3] *From Egyptian Rubbish-Heaps*, p. 43.

acute. [1] The Christian was in danger of pollution from two sources: (a) by accepting an invitation to dine in a Gentile house where meat might be served which had been sacrificed to an idol; (b) by purchasing in the open market meat which similarly might previously have been offered as a sacrifice in a heathen temple. The latitudinarian party in the Church at Corinth treated the issue as of small account. In their judgment an idol was nothing and had no power to harm. But another section of the Church lacked such knowledge and freedom. The idol was real and malignant. The participant was in imminent peril of falling into its evil power. To them the eating of meat which had been offered as a heathen sacrifice was anathema.

Paul is called upon to adjudicate. He does so in two sections of 1 Cor. In chap. viii. he deals with the problem from the point of view of the advanced members of the Church. Their duty, he urges, is to respect, even if they cannot accept, the fears of their weaker brethren. The idol is a nonentity, it is true. The conscientious scruples of the weaker members are therefore groundless. But nevertheless they must not be ruthlessly overridden. The guiding rule must be the spiritual development of the community, not the preferences of individual Christians. " Put no occasion of stumbling in the way of Jew or Gentile or the Church of God; that is my maxim."[2] Knowledge

---

[1] Cf. the resolution in Acts xv. 28–29. The matter of common meals would be crucial in the relations between Jew and Gentile in view of the strict table taboos among the Jews.

[2] MASSIE on Cor. (*Cent. B.*), p. 209.

and individual freedom must be limited by brotherly love. In chap. x. 14–22, Paul states the problem in a different way. Granted that the idol is nothing in itself, yet behind it is the living power of the demon, and to share in sacrifices offered to demons is radically incompatible with participation in a sacrifice offered to Christ. What is the root idea that lies behind this aspect of the case ? The basic notion inherent in the sacrificial meals of paganism was presumably the maintenance of communion between the brethren. H. A. A. KENNEDY [1] suggests that this is really based upon the fact of the deity's presence at the meal which he shares with the worshippers. So, for example, the phrase δειπνῆσαι εἰς κλείνην τοῦ κυρίου Σαράπιδος, " to dine at the table of the lord Serapis " (O.P. 523)—cf. ἡ τράπεζα τοῦ Κυρίου, " the table of the Lord " (1 Cor. x. 21) and Mal. i. 7, 12— implies nothing more than the presence of the deity at the sacred meal. The sacramental idea of communion with the god by feeding upon him is not here present. KENNEDY [2] says : " It is impossible, therefore, to bring forward any convincing evidence from Hellenistic religion contemporary with Paul in support of the conception of eating the god." There is indeed no direct evidence that this conception, assuming that it could be proved to have been the original idea underlying the sacrificial feast, survived in the Hellenistic world coeval with early Christianity.

In this light Paul's solution becomes more clear. As regards pagan feasts, the hosts, in his view,

[1] *St. Paul and the Mystery-Religions*, p. 259.
[2] *Ibid.*

are demons.[1] Cf. the phrase τράπεζα δαιμονίων, " table of demons " (1 Cor. x. 21).[2] It is not what a Christian eats, but the company he keeps and the hospitality he accepts, that decides the question. A Christian should not be the guest of demons. For the follower of Christ the legitimacy of the meal is contingent upon the character of the host. To eat at a heathen table is to commune with demons, and this is irreconcilable with communion with Christ in the Lord's Supper (1 Cor. x. 21). It is in this point, namely, that the *presence* of the deity at the meal gives it its sacramental character and *not* the actual eating of his body and drinking of his blood, that Paul's view of the Lord's Supper (*Κυριακὸν δεῖπνον*) shows kinship with the sacrificial meals of paganism. At the same time a further affinity between the Lord's Supper and the pagan ceremonial feasts must not be overlooked. In both the idea is implicit that " the worshippers, by partaking of the sacrifice, partook of the blessing which the sacrifice was to win."[3] The cup and the bread are means by which the Christian shares in the blessings Christ brought by the outpouring of His blood and the breaking of His body (1 Cor. x. 16–7).

2. In O.P. 114 the writer asks his friend to redeem various articles of attire held in pawn. Cf. Amos ii. 8. Two minæ was the amount of

---

[1] THACKERAY (*St. Paul*, etc., p. 146 f.) argues for Paul's view of the reality of the demonic power.

[2] Paul probably has in mind Deut. xxxii. 17 (cf. Psa. xcvi. 5 ; Baruch iv. 7).

[3] PLUMMER'S Art. *Lord's Supper*, in *H.D.B.*, vol. iii. p. 145 b.

the pledge, interest being charged at the rate of a stater per mina. Other letters illustrating the pawnbroking trade at Oxyrhynchus are 530 (a son sends money to his mother to redeem his wardrobe) and 936. The references suggest that Oxyrhynchus, though normally prosperous, was affected by the trade depression which afflicted the Fayûm district in the third century A.D.

3. O.P. 118 throws a gleam of light on the difficulties involved in travelling. Two travellers send for a ferry-boat " because of the uncertainty of the road." The " uncertainty " probably lay in the perils of brigandage as well as in the inadequate facilities for transit. Roads were good and fairly plentiful, it is true, but the wayside inns were often the haunt of highwaymen. Public security was insufficiently maintained. Paul speaks of himself as being " in journeyings often, in perils of rivers, in perils of robbers " (2 Cor. xi. 26). Cf. also in this respect the Parable of the Good Samaritan (Luke x. 30 ff.). RAMSAY [1] says " the roads all over the Roman Empire were apt to be unsafe, for the arrangements for insuring public safety were exceedingly defective." And again, " brigandage was rife, and brigands were followed in a very spiritless and variable way."[2] DEISSMANN [3] shows from a personal experience in April 1906 that " perils of robbers " still remain in the East. See also *Fayûm Towns and their Papyri*, No. 108.

4. Interesting peeps into human nature are

[1] *The Church in the Roman Empire*, p. 24.
[2] *Op. cit.*, p. 373.
[3] *L.A.E.*, p. 278, note 2.

afforded by many of these papyri. For example, in O.P. 121 (3/A.D.) we come across the following injunction. A certain Isidorus writes to his brother Aurelius, " don't allow the carpenters to be altogether idle. Worry them." The ca'canny policy is apparently no modern invention ! Cf. O.P. 1069, 19 where the writer says " make my slave girl be properly industrious." Cf. also O.P. 1493, 11 f. ; 1581, 5 ; 1682, 12 f. It is worth notice that Christianity lays emphasis upon the duty and dignity of work. Cf. 2 Thess. iii. 10. The Apostles toiled with their own hands, and the early Christians did not regard manual labour as ignominious.[1] The Founder of Christianity had worked at the carpenter's bench. ANGUS[2] says : " Work for wages and the winning of daily bread was distasteful, especially to the Greek and to the later Roman. The Greek ideal was a life of leisure freed from toil and care. The plunder of conquests inoculated the Roman with an aversion to hard work ; he loved *otium*, but it was no longer the well-earned rest. The Jew alone gave to toil an honourable place."

5. In O.P. 123 (3/4/A.D.) the writer expresses concern that a certain Timotheus, a notary, shall be properly robed to attend at court. " Our orders were to wear cloaks " (χλαμὺς).

---

[1] DEISSMANN (*L.A.E.*, p. 316 f.) thinks that in Paul's frequent references to ' labouring ' (Rom. xvi. 6, 12 ; 1 Cor. iv. 12, xv. 10 ; 1 Thess. iv. 11) his language is coloured by the fact of his intimate acquaintance with artisan toil. He had learned at Tarsus the local industry of tent-making (Acts xviii. 3, xx. 34–5).

[2] *The Environment of Early Christianity*, p. 35.

6. An interesting point arises in O.P. 294 (A.D. 22). Sarapion, who is about to engage in litigation, is urged by his friends to join the household of Apollonius, the chief usher, "in order that I may come to the session in his company." Association with an official's household apparently afforded advantages. If a man were a member of the household his lot stood more or less with that of his master. Cf. Matt. x. 25, where the οἰκιακοί share in the opprobrious epithet conferred upon their master (οἰκοδεσπότης). In P. Tebt. 34 (100 B.C.) it is urged that steps should be taken for the release of a debtor from prison on the ground that he was under the protection (ὑπὸ σκέπην) of a certain Demetrius, presumably an official of high standing. Cf. P. Tebt. 40.[1]

7. In O.P. 297 (A.D. 54) Ammonius asks his father to forward a supplementary return of lambs born since the first return of sheep for the year had been sent. Cf. O.P. 74 ; 246.

8. O.P. 744 (1 B.C.) is very significant for the light it sheds on the treatment of child-life in early Christian times. Hilarion, writing from Alexandria to his sister (wife) Alis says : " I beg and beseech you to take care of the little child." He then refers to her forthcoming accouchement. " If—good luck to you—you bear offspring, if it is a male, let it live ; if it is a female, expose it." The preference for a male child is here strongly marked (cf. also O.P. 1216, 14), and it may be presumed, from the father's solicitude, that the child already living was a boy. Exposure of female

[1] MILLIGAN'S *Selections*, p. 28, note 9.

infants was evidently fairly common in the Græco-Roman world. Cf. Acts vii. 21 (cf. Exod. ii. 3–10). A newly-born child would be placed at its father's feet. If it were unwanted, the father would not pick it up. It was then cast out. Cf. O.P. 37 (A.D. 49) which refers to the practice of women picking up foundlings from the dunghill and earning money by nursing them. There a certain Pesouris had rescued a male child from a dung-heap, and had entrusted it to the care of a nurse named Seraeus, who received a stated wage for her services.[1] Cf. O.P. 1069, 21 f., which WILCKEN suggests is a warning that the child must not be exposed. These references cast a lurid light on heathen society, and give point to Paul's judgment that it was " without natural affection " (Rom. i. 31, ἀστόργους). Infanticide by exposure was condemned by Justin Martyr (*Apol.* i. 27), and the *Epistle to Diognetus* (2/A.D.) boasts that Christians do not expose their children (v. 6).

The callousness of Hilarion's order is thrown into relief by the general tone of the letter, which is not unsympathetic. His attitude to his wife shows a certain rough kindness. But the child about to be born had apparently no claim. As GLOVER[2] says : " It is the kind of thing that we take for granted and assume to be normal that shows our character or gives the note of the day." It was a " hard pagan world " into which Christianity entered. The value set upon the child was largely utilitarian. As a potential citizen he was of value to the State. The teaching of Jesus

---

[1] MILLIGAN's *Selections*, p. 48 f.
[2] *The Jesus of History*, p. 66 f.

affords a striking contrast. He laid emphasis upon the intrinsic worth of the child (cf. Mark ix. 33 ff. ; Matt. xix. 13).

9. O.P. 930, 17 has the terms παιδαγωγός and καθηγητής. The former was the attendant, often a superior slave, who had charge of a boy till manhood. The latter was the teacher or instructor. H. A. A. KENNEDY[1] points out that the word καθηγητής preserves its meaning in M.Gr. (= ' professor '). Cf. the alternative reading in Matt. xxiii. 8. Paul describes the Law as a παιδαγωγὸς εἰς Χριστόν (Gal. iii. 24), that is, it was an agency for moral discipline among the Jews till they were fit for that fuller freedom with which Christ should set them free (cf. Gal. v. 1). In 1 Cor. iv. 15, the παιδαγωγός is contrasted with the father (πατήρ). PEAKE[2] says : " The office was temporary (until the child was sixteen), menial, and, of course, unpopular with its victims."

10. In O.P. 1068 (3/A.D.) there is a reference to the custom of carrying letters as a guarantee of safe and expeditious travelling. Cf. Acts ix. 2, xxii. 5, xxiii. 25 ; 1 Cor. xvi. 3.

11. MILLIGAN[3] finds in O.P. 1153, 3 ff. (1/A.D.) a reference to the practice of laying bundles of rolls in chests or arks. ἐκομισάμην διὰ ῾Ηρακλᾶτος τὰς κίστας (σὺν) τοῖς βιβλίοις, " I received through Heraclitus the chests with the books."

12. In O.P. 1157 (late 3/A.D.) the writer requests his sister to register him in his absence, if possible, and if not, to let him know that he may attend

[1] *Sources of N.T. Greek*, p. 153 ff.
[2] *Comm. on the Bible*, p. 836.
[3] *N.T.D.*, p. 20.

and register in person. The enrolment referred to in Luke ii. 2 (cf. Acts v. 37) is illustrated by the discovery among the papyri of many similar documents. In O.P. 1589 the writer speaks of an ἀπογραφή "enrolment," and hints at his coming to "Egypt." During the Imperial period a census was taken every fourteen years.[1] Cf. RAMSAY,[2] and GRENFELL and HUNT'S discussion.[3] In later times a return of property (e.g. slaves and cattle) was often included in the ἀπογραφή. See above, p. 139. Each person had to be registered according to his residence, a point which further illustrates Luke ii. 2 f. The discovery of enrolment documents among the non-literary papyri of Egypt bears directly upon the question of the historical accuracy of Luke ii. 1–4. MILLIGAN[4] has a careful discussion of census-returns.

13. In O.P. 1666 (3/A.D.) a sidelight is thrown upon Roman recruiting methods. A father applies at Alexandria to have his son transferred from a legion to serve in the cavalry. The application was successful.

C. Religious.

1. O.P. 115 (2/A.D.) is a touching letter of sympathy written by Irene to her friends Taonnophris and Philon, who have been bereaved of their son. The consolation offered is the more poignant in that Irene herself has known personal

---

[1] See *L.A.E.*, p. 268 ff.
[2] *Was Christ Born at Bethlehem ?*
[3] *O.P.* 254 (introd.).
[4] *Select.*, p. 44 f.

sorrow. But the note struck is that of Stoic acquiescence in what may befall. " Truly there is nothing anyone can do in the face of such things " (lines 9–10). The letter stands in striking contrast to the teaching of the N.T. on bereavement (cf. 1 Thess. iv. 14–18), which, as MILLIGAN [1] says, " the letter before us so strikingly recalls." DEISSMANN [2] thinks that set formulæ of consolation were current, and finds an example in the opening clauses of this letter. He suggests that Paul was acquainted with these stereotyped and conventional expressions of mourning. Some of his phrases appear to corroborate that view. For example, cf. 1 Thess. iv. 18 (ὥστε παρακαλεῖτε ἀλλήλους, " wherefore comfort one another ") with O.P. 115, 11 (παρηγορεῖτε οὖν ἑαυτούς, " comfort ye yourselves therefore ") ; cf. also 1 Thess. v. 11 and Heb. iii. 13. " St. Paul doubtless adopted the exhortation from the epistolary formulæ of the age." [3] ANGUS [4] points out that a new species of literature (" Consolations ") arose during the period of the early Empire and instances Cicero's *Consolatio*, Plutarch's *Consolation to his Wife* (on the loss of their infant daughter), and Seneca's *Consolation to Marcia*. The problem of pain and premature death was burdening the mind and heart of earnest men. " Consolatory formulæ were discovered for every calamity, for exile, old age, loss of health, physical suffering, confiscation of property, and chiefly for the death of friends."

[1] *Select.*, p. 96.
[2] *L.A.E.*, p. 164 ff.
[6] DEISSMANN'S *L.A.E.*, p. 167, note 3.
[4] *Environment*, etc., p. 129 f.

So Angus.[1] The attractiveness of the mystery-cults lay partly in the fact that they held out the promise of immortality for the "redeemed." It is noteworthy that in the present letter there is no hint of the hope of a hereafter.[2]

A kindred feature, namely, a fatalistic acquiescence in the inevitability of suffering and adversity, meets us in O.P. 120 (4/A.D.). A certain Hermias writes : "when a man finds himself in adversity he ought to give way and not fight stubbornly against fate. We fail to realise the inferiority and wretchedness to which we are born" (G.H.). But he ends on a more hopeful note : "we are resolved not to continue in misfortune." Men were obsessed with the thought that they were puppets in the hands of Chance (*Τυχή*) or Necessity ('*Ανάγκη*). Stoic teaching laid great stress upon the need of resignation to Fate which was, however, made subject to God's control. The general spirit of acquiescence in implacable destiny contrasts as strikingly with the teaching of Jesus (John xvi. 33) and Paul (Rom. v. 3, viii. 35 ; 2 Cor. vii. 4) as do the pessimism and *tædium vitæ* of the age with the hope and joy of early Christianity. Cf. the mournful note in Seneca and Lucretius.

2. A very common formula in the closing greetings of these letters is found in the term *ἀβασκάντως*, "unharmed by the evil eye" (cf. O.P. 292, 12 ; 930, 23, *al*). The superstition of the baleful influence of an "evil eye" was universal in the ancient

---

[1] *Environment*, etc., p. 130.

[2] The tone of the letter illustrates Paul's phrase "the rest, who have no hope" (1 Thess. iv. 13).

East. WHITEHOUSE [1] states that its origin is traditionally ascribed to Babylonia. It was not unknown among the Israelites (cf. Deut. xv. 9; xxviii. 54–6; Prov. xxiii. 6, xxviii. 22). Sorcerers (or more commonly witches) were supposed by means of the evil eye to control events or bind a malignant spell upon hapless individuals. Children and animals were specially liable, as possessing less power of resistance, to the evil influence. The N.T. references (Mark vii. 22 ; Matt. xx. 15) suggest that the idea of the malefic became weakened in course of time to that of envy or jealousy. The corresponding substantive (βασκανία) and verb (βασκαίνω) are used in Wisd. iv. 12 and Gal. iii. 1 respectively.

3. " Remember the night festival of Isis at the Serapeum." So writes the scribe of O.P. 525, 9. Ptolemy had introduced into Alexandria the cult of Serapis, who was identified with Osiris. Isis was both sister and wife of Osiris. The cult became a widely diffused syncretistic religion of the Hellenistic world. It was characterised by an imposing ritual, and it proclaimed the immortality of its devotees who shared in the divine life of Osiris.[2] Cf. O.P. 886, which is a magical formula addressed to Μεγάλη Ἶσις ἡ κυρία (" Great is the Lady Isis "), a phrase which at once calls to mind the Μεγάλη ἡ Ἄρτεμις Ἐφεσίων (" Great is Artemis (Diana) of the Ephesians ") of Acts xix. 28.

4. In O.P. 935, 9–11 (3/A.D.) Serenus, reporting the recovery of his sister from illness, says : " Our

[1] Art. *Sorcery*, in *H.D.B.*, vol. iv. p. 604 b.

[2] See H. A. A. KENNEDY's discussion in *St. Paul and the Mystery-Religions*, p. 95 ff.

ancestral gods continually assist us, granting us health and safety." Cf. also O.P. 936, 2 where a son, writing to his father, says : " I perform the act of worship on your behalf to the gods of the country." Cf. also O.P. 1296, 4 ; 1664, 5. There was a marked tendency among the ancients to transfer allegiance from their native gods to the gods of the land to which a man migrated. DEISS-MANN [1] remarks that a soldier will often worship the gods of the place where he happens to be garrisoned as assiduously as he had formerly served Serapis. The underlying idea was probably the view that the power of a deity was territorially confined. He had no place, and therefore no claim to service, in any land other than his own. That this conception was held at an early stage of Israelitish history seems clear from 1 Sam. xxvi. 19, where David, being driven by his enemies beyond the boundaries of Yahweh's land, deplores that he is excluded from the worship of Yahweh, but must " go " and " serve other gods." [2] In this connection it is interesting to note O.P. 1065, 6, " if you neglect this, as the gods have not spared me, so will I not spare the gods." The editors quote three passages (cf. O.P. 528, 10) which " illustrate the tendency in the popular religion to regard the relationship between gods and men as one of strict reciprocity. If the gods neglected their duty and afflicted their devotees, the sufferers retaliated by turning their backs on the gods." Faith in the gods was already in degree becoming undermined.

[1] *L.A.E.*, p. 173.
[2] See BURNEY's *Outlines of O.T. Theology*, p. 35.

5. Mention is made in O.P. 1161, 6 (a fourth-century Christian letter) of " body, soul and spirit " (σῶμα, ψυχή, πνεῦμα). The same tripartite division (though the constituents are set in a different order) is observable in 1 Thess. v. 23. Cf. also the implied differentiation between ' soul ' and ' spirit ' in Heb. iv. 12. ELLICOTT [1] favours trichotomy ; but MILLIGAN [2] enters a *caveat* : " this triple subject must not be pressed as if it contained a psychological definition of human nature." FINDLAY [3] leans to dichotomy. " The soul with Paul, as throughout Scripture, is not a *tertium quid* between spirit and flesh, but rather their unity, the living self behind the bodily form of each man." Similarly, H. A. A. KENNEDY,[4] following REITZENSTEIN, shows that in Philo and in a prayer of the Liturgy of Mithra ψυχή has assimilated the idea expressed by πνεῦμα, the human constitution being thus resolved into a dualism, ' soul ' versus ' body.' DAVID SMITH,[5] quoting Marcus Aurelius xii. 3, says that the threefold division of human nature is a Stoic conception.

6. O.P. 1161, 1162 (both dating from the fourth century A.D.) disclose a close parallelism to N.T. language which calls for brief mention. It may be well to cite the passage *in extenso* :—

1161, 2–6 : τῷ ἀγαθῷ ἡμῶν σωτῆρι καὶ τῷ υἱῷ αὐτου τῷ ἠγαπημένῳ ὅπως οὗτοι πάντες βοηθήσωσιν ἡμῶν τῷ σώματι, τῇ ψυχῇ, τῷ πνευματι, " To our

---

[1] *The Destiny of the Creature* (Sermon V).
[2] *Epp. to Thess.*, p. 78.
[3] Art. *Paul the Apostle*, in *H.D.B.*, vol. iii. p. 720.
[4] *St. Paul and the Mystery-Religions*, p. 142.
[5] *Life and Letters of St. Paul*, p. 166, note.

gracious Saviour and His beloved Son, that they all may succour our body, soul and spirit."

(a) The title ' Saviour ' as applied to God, is paralleled in Psa. cvi. 21 ; Isa. xliii. 3, xlv. 15 ; 1 Tim. i. 1, ii. 3 ; Tit. i. 3, ii. 10 *al* ; 2 Pet. i. 1 ; Jude 25 ; Luke i. 47. The N.T. usage of the title in reference to God and Christ takes on a deeper significance in the light of the fact that Roman Emperors were commonly hailed as Σωτήρ (e.g. the combination σωτήρ and θεός is used in reference to Augustus).[1] DEISSMANN [2] points out that the double ascription is as old as a votive offering at Halicarnassus in the third century B.C. which is dedicated to " Ptolemy the saviour and god." The term σωτήρ was also applied to the healing god Asclepius. The title accorded to Nero (σωτὴρ τῆς οἰκουμένης, " saviour of the earth ") [3] is in striking contrast to the language of John iv. 42 ; 1 John iv. 14.

(b) ἠγαπημένῳ (cf. ἀγαπητοῖς in O.P. 1162) is a well-marked Messianic title conferred upon Jesus (Matt. iii. 17 κ.τ.λ.). [4]

(c) σῶμα, ψυχή, πνεῦμα. See above, p. 147, note 5.

1162. Λέων πρεσβύτερος τοῖς κατὰ τόπον συν-λιτουργοῖς πρεσβυτέροις καὶ διακώνοις ἀγαπητοῖς ἀδελφοῖς ἐν κυρίῳ θεῷ, χαρᾷ χαίρειν. " Leon, presbyter, to the presbyters and deacons who share the local service, beloved brothers in the Lord God, fullness of joy."

---

[1] DEISSMANN's *L.A.E.*, p. 348, note 4.

[2] *Op. cit.*, p. 349.

[3] *Archiv.* 11, p. 434.

[4] See J. ARM. ROBINSON's excursus in *Comm. on Eph.*, p. 229 ff.

(a) πρεσβύτερος. The title applied originally to the holders of a civil office. Later it developed a definitely ecclesiastical connotation and signified 'elders' who had oversight in the primitive Christian societies. So DEISSMANN.[1]

(b) διάκονος, ἀδελφὸς ἐν κυρίῳ θεῷ, χαρᾷ χαίρειν (cf. John iii. 29) are strongly reminiscent of N.T. language.

1494, 9 : ὁδὸς εὐθεῖα. Cf. the exact parallel in 2 Pet. ii. 15. Cf. also Mark i. 3 ; Acts ix. 11.

1495. In this Christian letter the Biblical contractions of κύριος (also in O.P. 1493, and 1592) and θεός occur.[2]

Three Biblical proper names may be noted in passing : Τύραννος (Acts xix. 9 ; O.P. 292 ; 746 ; 937), Ἐμμανουήλ (Isa. vii. 14; viii. 8 ; Matt. i. 23 ; O.P. 1162, 14) and Θεόφιλος (Luke i. 3 ; Acts i. 1 ; O.P. 745, 4).

In this connection of presumed Christian influence an allusion in O.P. 1299, 6 (4/A.D.) may be cited. "Up to the present we have not sacrificed the pigs." COBERN[3] hazards the conjecture that the reference is to a common heathen sacrifice, and that the writers wish to indicate that they are standing firm in the Christian Faith, and that so far they have successfully withstood any reversion to their former pagan practices and manner of life.

The question of the relation between Christianity and contemporary mystery religions, though not

---

[1] B.S., pp. 154, 233 ff.

[2] For other examples of Christian influence see above, p. 126.

[3] New Archæological Discoveries, p. 321.

directly raised by any reference in these papyrus-letters, may nevertheless be briefly mentioned under this section. The extent of the formative influence of Oriental cults upon Pauline Christianity is one of the live questions of modern N.T. research. Two extremes need to be avoided.

1. It cannot be claimed that there is no affinity between primitive Christianity and the syncretistic religions of its Hellenistic environment. On the face of it such remoteness would be incredible on at least two grounds. For one thing, Christianity is a historical religion. Its origin and early development, its outlook and religious contribution can only be adequately understood as the movement itself is set in the whole context of the age in which it arose. That age was one of an extraordinary religious quest. National and ancestral faiths had failed. The mind of the West hungered for a new knowledge, its heart craved a new fellowship. There was patent need of guidance in the moral life. Men lacked the moral strength to realise the moral ideal. They sought a new way of life. Similarly, in the realm of spirit there was a feeling after authority. Something of the nature of religious faith was desiderated to meet that which the rational had obviously failed to satisfy. There was a yearning for salvation (σωτηρία), a demand for a universal religion which should fully meet the needs of awakened personality. As often in human history, light appeared in the East. ANGUS [1] says: " Of the religions competing in the Empire, those of Greece were philo-

_____
[1] _Environment_, etc., p. 84.

sophical, appealing primarily to the reason and
intellect ; that of Rome was wholly political ;
those from the Orient were most akin to Christianity, making their appeal primarily to the heart."
The East was the home of a medley of cults which
made by their mysticism and emotionalism an
enormous appeal to the Græco-Roman world.
Among these, Isis and Serapis were characteristic
of Egypt, as Mithra (which made large conquests
among the Roman soldiery) was of Persia. It
cannot reasonably be maintained that Christianity
was unaffected by the complex of religious idea
and aspiration that characterised its time. Being
in its age, it must necessarily have been, in the
best sense, of its age. Moreover, for apologetic
purposes alone it would be necessary for the
exponents of early Christianity to live in the
thought-world of Hellenism. Paul doubtless speaks
for them all when he says, " I am become all
things to all men, that I may by all means save
some."[1] In the nature of the case the advocate
must begin by finding common ground with his
hearer. HARNACK's theory [2] that the author of
the Fourth Gospel was himself not specially inter-
ested in, though he accepted the truth of, the
Logos idea (the term is confined to the Prologue),
but placed it in the forefront of his work in order
to attract Greek readers to whom this conception
was both familiar and congenial, has not found
general acceptance. But it has at least the merit
of probability. One can readily conceive that the

[1] 1 Cor. ix. 22.
[2] *On the Relation of the Prologue of the Fourth Gospel to
the Whole Work* (1892).

writer of the Fourth Gospel might accord a prominent place to his philosophic Prologue in order
to win a hearing from the Greek world. The
same method of apologetic tactics may be illustrated from the speeches in Acts. Paul's oration
on Mars Hill (Acts xvii. 22 ff.) is a case in point.
He starts from the Athenian point of view (" an
unknown god ") only to advance upon it. The
Apostolic sensitiveness to the current philosophical and religious atmosphere is illustrated by
both the thought and the language of early
Christian books. H. A. A. KENNEDY [1] points out
that Paul's description of the cosmic significance
of Christ shows "intimate affinities with ten-
dencies of thought current in contemporary Hellenistic speculation." He notes especially the prepositional phrases "by him," "through him,"
"for him," "in him," which are closely paralleled
in the current philosophic language. Cf. also Paul's
use of συνέστηκεν in Col. i. 17 with Περὶ Κόσμου, 6,
which shows many traces of Stoic influence.[2] Cf.
also συνείδησις (" conscience ") and τὰ μὴ καθήκοντα
(" the things that are not fitting ") (see above
pp. 59 f. and 47 respectively) as analogous cases
which have emerged during the present enquiry.
In these and other instances Paul's language
touches that of popular Stoic moral teaching.[3]
This is only what we might expect from one who

[1] *The Theology of the Epistles*, p. 155.

[2] See KENNEDY, *op. cit.*, p. 155.

[3] It is not a necessary inference that Paul had made
a special study of Stoic literature. Stoic terms had per-
meated the ethical vocabulary of the age and would be
commonly known.

grew up in a Hellenised city and laboured in a Hellenistic environment.

2. But the assertion that prominent features of Christian theology have been shaped by Eastern mystery-cults is an exaggeration not warranted by the facts. H. A. A. KENNEDY [1] has dealt searchingly with the whole question. His general judgment is that more allowance should be made, in estimating the origin of Christian tenets, for the more immediate background of Christianity, viz. the Old Testament, and that what is distinctive of Pauline Christianity derives from that profound experience of conversion and union with Christ which was granted to its author. Where resemblances between Paulinism and the mystery-cults appear, as, for example, in such notions as ' knowledge of God ' and ' redemption,' the implications show fundamental differences. The mystery-cults proclaimed redemption from inexorable fate ; Paul preached redemption from sin. The Pauline $\gamma\nu\hat{\omega}\sigma\iota\varsigma$ " knowledge " was attainable not by unaided effort and through mystic ritual, but by a co-operative faith in the crucified Christ leading to a life of earnest moral effort sustained by His aid (cf. Phil. iv. 13). In Paulinism it is supremely necessary to distinguish the essential message from that which accidentally accompanies it. Paul's originality lay not in entire independence of the thought of his age (even if such a mental detachment were possible), but in the transformation into higher values of the permanent element in Hellenistic religions. What was good and true he did not disdain to bring into the service of the

[1] *St. Paul and the Mystery-Religions.*

Gospel. But Paulinism is Paul. The distinctive religious contribution of the Apostle was formed in the matrix of his own rich experience of redemption from sin and conscious union with the Living Lord (cf. his pregnant phrase "in Christ"). The interpretation set upon that experience by his religious genius found articulate expression, as we should expect, in terminology which reflected the moral and spiritual aspirations of his time.

D. Miscellaneous.

1. In O.P. 113, 23 (2/A.D.) the writer asks for a silver seal. The allusions to seals and sealing in these papyrus-letters are numerous, and apparently refer to a very common practice in the ancient East. Seals took various forms, e.g scarab, signet. The substance on which the impression was stamped was usually wax or prepared clay. Cf. O.P. 929, 13 (a brown tunic containing various domestic articles is sealed with white clay), and Job xxviii. 14. B. GRENFELL [1] thinks that the custom of sealing papyrus documents in Egypt dates from very early times. The main ideas signified by sealing were :

(*a*) Security. A letter or parcel would be sealed so as to preserve its contents inviolable, the supposition being that if the seal were broken it could not easily and safely be replaced. So the stone at the mouth of the lion's den (Dan. vi. 17) was sealed. Cf. also Matt. xxvii. 66. This seems to be the prevailing idea in the present papyrus references, e.g. O.P. 116, 20 (fruit sent off ' under

[1] See *H.D.B.*, vol. iv. p. 426, footnote.

seal '), 117, 15 (two strips of cloth ' sealed with my seal '), 528 (a letter despatched through a messenger is ' sealed '), 1062 (delivery under seal of some fleeces). Cf. further O.P. 121 ; 932 ; 1293 ; 1677. There is a suggestive instance in O.P. 1067. A sister (Helene) writes to announce her brother's death. Evidently bearing in mind his testamentary dispositions ("a strange woman will be his heir ") she remarks, " a cellar has been sealed up although he owes nothing," the allusion probably being to the practice of sealing and so safeguarding goods as an indemnification against debt. Closely akin to the thought of security is that of the secrecy of that which is sealed. Cf. Rev. x. 4 ; xxii. 10.

(*b*) Authentication. Jezebel, for example, wrote letters under Ahab's seal (1 Kings xxi. 8). In Roman law a will had to be sealed by seven witnesses. The will could not be executed until the seals were broken. When a document was drawn up and seals were affixed, its validity was complete. Cf. Neh. x. 1 ; Jer. xxxii. 14. Some scholars (e.g. HUSCHKE, ZAHN) regard the " book written within and on the back, close sealed with seven seals " (Rev. v. 1) as a will. Cf. the further references in Rev. vi. 3 ; vii. 2 ; viii. 1 ; ix. 4. MILLIGAN, [1] however, prefers to see in the ' seven ' of Rev. v. 1 merely the Jewish sacred number. Again, it is not a far remove from the idea of authentication to that of possession, and this seems to be dominant in 2 Tim. ii. 19. Cf. also 1 Cor. ix. 2 ; Rom. iv. 11 ; Eph. i. 13 ; 2 Cor. i. 22.

[1] *N.T.D.*, p. 17.

Hence, in the papyri " sealing " usually signified imperial protection and legalisation. COBERN [1] points out that seals were affixed, e.g. to sacks of corn to guarantee the correctness of their contents. A mark (χάραγμα) was placed on documents of buying and selling, and this mark was known as the ' seal.' Cf. Rev. xiii. 16, 17 ; xiv. 9, 11. MASSIE [2] agrees that some such idea underlies Rom. xv. 28. Paul has in mind the formalities proper to a commercial transaction. He guarantees that what he hands over is the correct amount due from him. " The suspicions which some of his enemies had set afloat, that he helped himself from the collection, must be definitely and completely foreclosed."

2. In O.P. 531, 10 (2/A.D.) a father shows anxiety on the score of his son's studies, and gives him the following good advice : τοῖς βιβλίοις σου αὐτὸ μόνον πρόσεχ[ε] φιλολογῶν καὶ ἀπ'αὐτῶν ὄνησιν ἕξεις, " Give your sole attention to your books with love of learning, and you will have profit from them." Cf. 1 Tim. iv. 13.

3. In a letter to his mother (O.P. 839—early first century) a certain Eutychides speaks of a shipwreck at Ptolemais. We are reminded of Paul's phrase, " thrice I suffered shipwreck, a night and a day have I been in the deep." Among the perils he endured were those " in the sea " (2 Cor. xi. 25–26). Cf. the graphic description given in Acts xxvii. 9 ff.

4. In O.P. 1489, 3 (3/A.D.) we read that a certain Sattos, having left behind a cloak (κιθών), asks

---

[1] *New Archæological Discoveries*, p. 36 f.
[2] Art. *Seal*, in *H.D.B.*, vol. iv. p. 427 a.

that it shall be delivered to a hairdresser. The case of Paul leaving behind his cloak (φελόνης) at Troas comes to mind (2 Tim. iv. 13). In O.P. 1583 (2/A.D.) we read of the writer sending for a cloak (φαινόλης), and in O.P. 1584 (2/A.D.) of φαινολίων ζεύγη β (" two pairs of cloaks ").

CHAPTER VII

CONCLUSION

THE nature of our enquiry precludes the possibility of reaching from the facts adduced some
all-embracing conclusion. The fragmentary character of the papyri imposes a distinct limitation.
Moreover, as we have emphasised, the area in
which evidence has been sought is circumscribed.
All inductions, therefore, especially those of a
philological character, need to be tested by data
drawn from other fields. In the lexical and
grammatical portions of this essay nothing more
has been attempted than to glean a few materials
of interest and significance for N.T. language after
the manner adopted by MILLIGAN in his *Selections
from the Greek Papyri*. All, therefore, that we can
now hope to do is to co-ordinate, as far as possible,
the evidence that has accrued, to see what is its
purport and drift, and to discover how far it
confirms or modifies general conclusions based
upon all relevant sources. It may be necessary
to emphasise and supplement the evidence at
various points. This chapter aims at setting
forth simply and briefly the results of our investigation as they affect the N.T. in (1) its linguistic

character, (2) its epistolary forms, and (3) its cultural environment.[1]

1. What light do the linguistic data of these papyri throw on the character of N.T. Greek? At this point, the question of Semitisms arises. (The term 'Semitisms' is here used to cover Hebrew, the language of the O.T., and Aramaic, which supplanted Hebrew as the mother-tongue of the Jews.) In the main, three theories have been held : (a) that N.T. Greek is strictly classical, its supposed peculiarities being discoverable in 'profane' writings. This Purist position is now entirely untenable. It probably drew what force it possessed from a view of inspiration which is no longer widely entertained. Moreover, as we have stated in our sketch of the origin and place of the κοινή in the development of the Greek tongue (*vide supra*, p. 15 f.), the post-classical and late Greek showed marked differences from its Attic predecessor, especially in vocabulary, compounds and combinations being specially common. (For grammatical differences see Appendix II). (b) That the idiom of the N.T. is of Semitic cast. The Hebraist school hold that the writers of the N.T. were influenced by LXX Greek (which was an over-literal translation of the O.T. Hebrew), and by Aramaic (the writers either translated from Aramaic sources or thought and spoke in Aramaic). Hence the Greek of the N.T. was deemed an isolated species of the language, 'Biblical Greek.' In the words of BLASS,[2] it " is to be

[1] The palæographical and orthographical significance of the papyri have been briefly intimated on pp. 23, 91 ff.

[2] Quoted by DEISSMANN in Art. *Papyri*, in *Encyc. Bib.*, col. 3561.

regarded as something by itself and following laws of its own." [1] The fact that it could not be paralleled from the literary κοινή of the period (from Plutarch or Philo, etc.) lent colour to the view. (c) That the Greek of the N.T. is simply the vernacular of its own day, the language of ordinary conversation.

The finding of immense numbers of papyri and inscriptions gives ample warrant for the third theory. DEISSMANN'S epoch-making discovery in 1895 was anticipated by both MASSON [2] in 1859 and LIGHTFOOT [3] in 1863. In the light of the new evidence the Hebraist position whilst not by any means wholly discredited must be largely qualified. The papyri in particular establish the fact that the language of the N.T. is one with the κοινή of the Hellenistic world.[4] Paul's words, for example, can be paralleled from vernacular sources. The same holds true of the Gospels, though in less degree. Their language is more fettered. Aramaic originals lay behind the Gospels (and probably also behind parts of the Book of Acts), and in consequence the Evangelists were affected by the diction of their sources. The data presented in the linguistic portions of this essay (Chapters III and IV) point in the same direction. Taken as a whole the evidence examined, limited as it is, tends to confirm the general judgment of modern

---

[1] DEISSMANN (B.S., pp. 174–175) points out that BLASS, in his *Grammar*, abandoned that extreme position.

[2] ROBERTSON'S *Grammar*, p. xii.

[3] MOULTON'S *Prolegomena*, p. 242.

[4] DEISSMANN (L.A.E., p. 73) estimates that out of 5,000 N.T. words only 50 or less can be reckoned as " Biblical Greek " words.

scholarship in respect to the native character of
N.T. Greek. See notes (*passim*). Only the chief
possible Semitisms have been noted. They are
practically confined to less than a dozen instances,
namely, ἐρωτάω (p. 57), ἀρραβών (p. 58), τρία τρία
(p. 85 f.), ἰδού (p. 71 f.), redundant personal pronoun
(p. 73 f.), ἐν τῷ with the infinitive (p. 80 f.), ἀριθμῷ
(p. 77 f.). Of these ἐρωτάω and ἀριθμῷ are probably
to be ruled out (see notes *in loco*). τρία τρία, ἰδού,
and the redundant personal pronoun may be
deemed only ' secondarily ' Hebraic, that is, the
frequency of these locutions in Greek is due to
the fact that they answer to an equivalent construction in Hebrew.   This leaves ἀρραβών and
ἐν τῷ with the infinitive, which may be regarded
as ' genuine ' Semitisms.

At the same time the disavowal of a ' Biblical '
kind of Greek must not be made too dogmatically.
The influence of translation from Aramaic, the
fact of Aramaic mentality and speech among some
of the N.T. writers, and of their unconscious
reminiscences of LXX language, are factors in the
case which must not be minimised. Semitisms
are undoubtedly to be found in the N.T. What
scholarship still has to define is their range and
relative proportion. Scholars of repute think that
DEISSMANN and MOULTON have moved too far
in free elimination of Semitic elements in the
language of the Greek Testament.   OTTLEY [1]
says : " It must not be taken for granted that
the κοινή was entirely free from Semitic influence ;
and when close parallels to Semitic forms of
speech appear in translations from Hebrew and

[1] *Handbook to the Septuagint*, p. 166.

in the writings of Jews and close associates of Jews, it requires the strongest of proofs to fortify the assertion that such parallels are due to natural development of the Greek itself, and not to imitation, or influence of the Semitic idiom." MILLIGAN [1] also calls for caution.

A further point invites brief notice. It has been suggested by SWETE [2] that " the quasi-Semitic colloquialisms of the (Egyptian) papyri " arise from the fact that Aramaic-speaking Jews settled in large numbers in the Delta of the Nile, the implication being that such turns of speech were not native but imported. OTTLEY [3] suggests that some of the papyri may have been written by Jews. The fact that there was a large Jewish population in Egypt must be freely admitted. But it has not yet been proved that their presence accounts for the supposed Semitic strain in the phraseology of the Græco-Egyptian papyri. For the testimony of the latter does not stand alone. In many cases, both lexical and grammatical papyrus usages are confirmed by the vernacular inscriptions of different countries where undue Semitic influence cannot be presupposed. MOULTON [4] brings out this point clearly in the case of the instrumental ἐν. It is as yet an unproved hypothesis that Egyptian Greek was coloured by Semitisms to an appreciably greater extent than that spoken throughout the Empire. ROBERTSON [5]

[1] *Selections*, p. xxx, notes 1, 2.
[2] *The Apocalypse of St. John*, p. cxx.
[3] *Handbook*, p. 165.
[4] *Proleg.*, p. xvii.
[5] *Grammar*, p. 56.

says : " The papyri and the inscriptions prove beyond controversy that the Greek tongue was practically the same whether in Egypt, Herculaneum, Pergamum or Magnesia."

The acceptance of the thesis that the language of the N.T. is not a distinct entity but is typical in the main of the ordinary colloquial speech of its day must not hide the fact that in a very real sense the sacred writers had a language of their own. Their work was not so much to coin new words as to enrich old ones. No objection need be taken to the term " N.T. Greek " if, by its use, it is recognised that the authors gave the vocabulary they found in common currency a new and richer meaning. Workaday words were filled with a deeper content. We have met several examples in the course of the present enquiry. See notes on παρουσία (p. 58), συνείδησις (p. 59), ἀδελφή (p. 61), σωτηρία (p. 62). We have also seen that terms used by Stoic moral teachers assume a richer and fuller significance on the lips of Paul. MOULTON [1] reminds us pertinently that " the N.T. must still be studied largely by light drawn from itself." The setting of the N.T. Scriptures in their historical linguistic connections, so far from impairing their peculiar genius which BLASS [2] so strongly and rightly stressed; serves only to throw it into stronger relief. The high themes with which the N.T. deals (and these necessarily find reflection in heightened and enriched language) accord it a distinction all its own. (On Semitisms in the N.T. see Appendix I.)

2. Warning is also needed against inferring

[1] *Proleg.*, p. 20.
[2] See DEISSMANN's *B.S.*, p. 174 f.

from the colloquial character of N.T. Greek that
it is destitute of literary quality. It is no mere
vulgar speech. ROBERTSON[1] says : " The N.T.
uses the language of the people, but with a dignity,
restraint, and pathos far beyond the trivial nonen-
tities in much of the papyri remains." The best
N.T. examples of popular Greek are probably to
be found in the Synoptic Gospels (especially in
Mark, which probably comprises shorthand notes
of Peter's addresses), and the speeches in Acts.
Paul's letters, too, as we have seen, are couched
in the everyday vernacular. But there are strata
in the N.T. which evince a distinctly literary
quality, e.g. Luke i. 1–4 ; Acts i. 1–5 ; Rom. viii. ;
Eph. iii. ; Heb. ; 2 Pet. ; Jas. ; Jude ; and Paul's
speeches on Mars Hill and before Agrippa
(Acts xvii. 22 ff. ; xxvi. 2 ff.). In these sections
are found not only a number of good classical
forms and constructions, but also words which
belong definitely to the language of literary culture.
2 Peter especially savours of bookish Greek.
Where the occasion demanded it correct and
polished language would naturally be used (assuming that the author had it at his command) rather
than the colloquial idiom. BLASS[2] finds the
following literary traces in Paul's speech before
Agrippa (where he had a cultured audience) :—

> Acts xxvi. 14, πρὸς κέντρα λακτίζειν.
> ,, xxvi. 26, οὐκ ἐστιν ἐν γωνίᾳ, κ.τ.λ.
> ,, xxvi. 4, ἴσασιν (instead of οἴδασιν) cf. ἴστε
>   for οἴδατε in James i. 19.

[1] *Grammar*, p. 84.
[2] *Grammar of N.T. Greek*, p. 5.

Acts xxvi. 5, the superlative in τὴν ἀκριβεστάτην αἵρεσιν.

MOULTON [1] points out that " there was a fondness for obsolete words with literary associations," and instances ναῦς (Acts xxvii. 41). The language of the N.T. is, in the main, that of daily life. It is colloquial Greek. But it is not without traces of true literary excellence, e.g. the Parable of the Prodigal Son (Luke xv. 11 ff.) and Paul's Hymn of Love (1 Cor. xiii.). It would be passing strange were it otherwise when we recall what manner of men contributed to its pages. Even in the case of the early disciples sufficient allowance has not always been made for the intellectual enrichment which must necessarily have formed a part of the spiritual fellowship with Jesus that they enjoyed. Would they not gain educationally (in the best sense of the word) by association with Jesus ? The Twelve were appointed " that they might be with him " (Mark iii. 14). Great diversity of culture existed among the N.T. writers (cf. Acts iv. 13), but it will not be denied that Paul, Luke, and the unidentified author(ess) of the Epistle to the Hebrews were people of education. Paul shows some degree of familiarity with Greek poets (in Acts xvii. 28 he quotes from Aratus and Cleanthes, cf. also 1 Cor. xv. 33 ; Titus i. 12), and was not unacquainted with Stoic philosophy. Luke's language is that of an educated writer of the κοινή interspersed with medical terms.[2] The author of Hebrews shows unmistakably the influence of

---

[1] *Proleg.*, p. 25.
[2] See HOBART'S *The Medical Language of Luke.*

Alexandrian culture. If the literary quality of parts of the N.T. books is restrained and strictly subordinate to the practical and ethical needs of their original readers, the language is characterised by a simplicity, directness and grace which must not be overlooked in estimating its worth as literature. DEISSMANN's statement [1] that Paul's Greek " never becomes literary " is extreme. It would become such more often but for the Apostle's determined effort to keep his message within the range of the common people.[2] But now and again real literary grace shines through (cf. 1 Cor. xv.). Similar occasional literary intrusions are discernible even in the papyri, and much more markedly in the official inscriptions the language of which is often formal and artificial.

The best criterion of the literary quality of any part of the N.T. is probably to be found in the circumstances under which it was spoken or written. The fact that the N.T. authors wrote under the belief that the *Parusia* would not be long delayed, and therefore addressed themselves to an immediate or imminent situation, should always be borne in mind. Paul's letters, for example, are casual in character. They were not written as permanent literature. It may be of interest to notice a theory propounded by HARNACK [3] respecting a literary test. His general position is that Matthew has more faithfully preserved Q than has Luke, the latter resorting

[1] *L.A.E.*, p. 64.

[2] It is the practical aim of Paul that largely accounts for the popular language of his letters.

[3] *Sayings of Jesus*, pp. 84 ff., 150 ff.

constantly to stylistic corrections. A point in the case is that the use of compound verbs is indicative of literary culture. HARNACK instances ἐπιλελησμένον (Luke xii. 6), and Luke's employment of παραγίνεσθαι (Luke xii. 51) instead of the simple ἐλθεῖν (Matt. x. 34), as marking " the language of literature." [1] But these supposed signs of Lucan refinement are not wanting in the papyri. Cf. ἐπιλαθεῖν in O.P. 744, 12 ; 1481, 3. The fact is, as MOULTON [2] says : " The increased use of compounds was one of the features of the κοινή as compared with classical Greek, and applied to literary and vernacular language alike." Mark uses compounds freely, and he, together with the author of Revelation, with its grammatical irregularities and unusual vocabulary, is the least cultured of the N.T. writers. It would seem, therefore, that the presence of compounds cannot be accepted as a satisfactory test of literary style, [3] and that HARNACK's preference in many passages for Matthew (who distinctly favours the simple form of verbs) as against Luke cannot be justified on this ground.

3. So far as our investigation has thrown light upon the letter-form of portions of the N.T. the results may be briefly summarised.

(a) The prevalence of the epistolary element in all the chief papyri collections points to the fact that the writing of letters was a general practice of the Græco-Roman age (see above p. 35).

[1] *Sayings of Jesus*, pp. 84, 86.
[2] *Grammar*, vol. ii. p. 11.
[3] See MOULTON's Art. in *Camb. Bib. Essays*, p. 492 ff., and art. on *Some Criticisms of Professor Harnack's " Sayings of Jesus,"* in *Expositor*, May 1909.

(*b*) Paul's writings, it would appear, provide the first and clearest example of the use of the letter as a means of religious didacticism and edification (see above, p. 103 f.).

(*c*) In general form and structure, in epistolary phrase and formula, the letters of the N.T. are identical with the secular correspondence of their own period. The forms of the Greek epistolary style which have emerged in the course of the present investigation form a body of evidence which, though drawn from a limited area, points to the fact that Paul's language in particular is largely that of the secular epistolary writings of his day. Now and again there is a distinct flavour of religio-philosophical terms. It is probably true, as H. A. A. KENNEDY holds [1] that Paul had no intimate acquaintance with Hellenistic mystery literature, but he did not scruple to use on occasion the liturgical and technical formulæ associated with the cultus of his age. Into the current speech, whether of the street or of the schools, Paul poured heightened and sacred meaning, but the mould was that of his Hellenistic environment. Only with this point in mind can we accept FINDLAY's statement [2] that " St. Paul has no hackneyed formulæ." It was the connotation that was new (see above, p. 113 f.)

(*d*) But kinship in other respects is not so thoroughly established. Whereas the O.P. are obviously " true letters," the same cannot be said, without serious qualification, of the N.T. Epistles. As we have seen (*supra*, p. 96 ff.), the

[1] *St. Paul and the Mystery-Religions*, pp. 117–118.
[2] *The Epistles of Paul the Apostle*, p. 37.

latter do not easily fall within the confines of DEISSMANN'S clear-cut division, 'letter' and 'epistle.'

(e) Further, whilst the Pauline writings are true letters in their strongly marked personal element (*supra*, p. 97 ff.), they have added and distinctive qualities in their religious aim and spiritual content, their occasional traces of careful preparation and evidences of literary grace, and their semi-publicity. These features separate them from the class of ordinary letters.

(f) Lastly, the N.T. Epistles as a whole are *sui generis*. Loftiness of theme and intensity of religious passion mark their uniqueness as they constitute also their crowning glory.

4. The following brief statement comprises the main points relative to the cultural environment of early Christianity which have issued from our enquiry.

(a) The Egyptian papyri are of special value for our knowledge of the history of the period which they cover (roughly a thousand years). (See p. 26.)

(b) They confirm in some important particulars the historical reliability of the N.T. (see above, p. 142).

(c) The papyri in general, and especially the private letters, reflect the thought and speech of the lower classes amongst whom Christianity mainly made its converts.

(d) The artlessness and unconscious self-portraiture of these ancient letter-writers show that human nature is substantially the same in all ages. The family letters, which so largely preponderate, afford strong ground for this conclusion.

The alternation of hope and fear, the wistfulness of desire, the poignancy of sorrow and the elation of success—all in these letters that makes " the still, sad music of humanity "—awakes an echo in our hearts. It is this fact which lends to many of these papyrus letters their striking modernity (see above, p. 137 f.).

(*e*) Primitive Christianity stood in intimate relation with the thought currents of its age. The papyri illuminate the N.T. in some points ; in others they suggest likely explanations of obscure references. There are distinct points of contact. See, for example, in these papyri the allusions to bathing, branding, pagan feasts, etc. But even more striking are the points of contrast, e.g. the attitude to bereavement, the meaning and purpose of suffering (*supra*, p. 142 ff.), the conception of personality. See especially the treatment of child-life (*supra*, p. 139 ff.). In thought, the difference between the N.T. and the papyri-remains is tremendous. In the latter the thought is often as mundane and shallow as in the former it is lofty and spiritual. In the light of these facts it becomes abundantly clear that early Christianity stood over against its time in sharp relief. Whilst the religion of Jesus borrowed the thought-forms and spoke the language of its day, it was as original in its essential message as it was in its inherent character. In the nature of the case it could not remain unaffected by Paganism, Platonism, Stoicism and the Mystery cults. Yet it advanced immeasurably upon any and all of these. It was not a syncretistic religion. Christianity is explained not by its pagan environment, but by its historical emergence from Judaism into a new and revolutionary movement centring in the Person of its Founder. The originality of Apostolic Christianity is clearly seen when it is viewed as a whole. The papyri, in so far as they cast light upon its religious and philosophical conditions, confirm this judgment.

APPENDIX I

SOURCES OF SEMITISMS IN N.T. WRITERS

MOULTON[1] classifies Semitisms as :

1. ' Secondary.' These arise mainly as (*a*) cases of ' over-use,' due to a literal rendering producing a phrase which ordinarily is not of frequent use in good Greek. It becomes of more common use because it answers to some word or phrase in Semitic, e.g. ἰδού and ἐνώπιον.[2] These cases are quite genuine Greek, but they are secondarily Semitic in that their relative frequency is due to the fact that they correspond to that which is common in the language from which the translation derives. (*b*) Cases in which words in Semitic bearing a special metaphorical meaning are translated into the Greek that literally corresponded to it, e.g. הָלַךְ in its ethical sense (" walk rightly ") was rendered, not by its equivalent ἀναστρέφεσθαι, but by περιπατεῖν (cf. 1 Pet. iv. 3).[3] Cases of (*b*) are relatively few. The majority belong to (*a*).

2. ' Genuine.' These originate in (*a*) imitation (conscious or otherwise) of LXX Greek (Hebraisms), (*b*) literal renderings from Aramaic originals (as,

---

[1] *Proleg.*, p. 10 f. ; *Gram.*, vol. ii. p. 14 f.
[2] *Gram.*, vol. ii. p. 15.
[3] *Proleg.*, p. 11.

for example, in the Synoptists and parts of Acts), and renderings due to thinking in Aramaic and writing in Greek (Aramaisms).

A further distinction should also be drawn between grammatical Semitisms on the one hand and lexical on the other. The latter belong, according to DEISSMANN,[1] "mostly to the technical language of religion." The former constitute a dwindling quantity before the evidence yielded by the papyri, which shows many instances of grammatical violations hitherto reputed to be Semitisms. Moreover, the N.T. authors were bilingual. They knew both Aramaic (except perhaps Luke [2] and the writer of Hebrews) and Greek.[3] Paul, especially, was well versed in both tongues (cf. Acts xxii. 2 ; Phil. iii. 5). Mark and the author of the Apocalypse were apparently deficient in their knowledge of Greek. At the other end of the scale stand the writers of 1 Peter, James, and Jude, who show marked facility in their handling of the Greek language. MOULTON [4] makes much of the linguistic difference between Jerusalem and Galilee. Northern Palestine, which housed a large Gentile population, was strongly bilingual. Greek would be a common medium of communication. It is not improbable, therefore, that Jesus abandoned his usual Aramaic for Greek, especially when moving in North Pales-

[1] Quoted in *Proleg.*, p. 18.

[2] So JÜLICHER (*Introd.*, p. 359) and DALMAN (*Words of Jesus*, pp. 38–41).

[3] It is significant that it is in the writings of Luke, the only non-Jewish contributor, that the problem of N.T. Semitisms is most complicated.

[4] *Gram.*, vol. ii. p. 12 f.

tinian circles. Some of the parables, MOULTON thinks, may have been originally uttered in Greek.[1] So he holds it natural that the writings of the Galileans (1 Peter, James, Jude) should exhibit a free and easy Greek idiom. Mark, as a dweller in Jerusalem, shows a very inadequate grasp of Greek. His Gospel is rich in Aramaisms.

The probable sources of Semitisms in the chief N.T. writers may be briefly indicated thus :—

Auctor ad Hebraeos.

Semitisms are due to the influence of the LXX, of which the writer reveals an intimate knowledge.

Paul.

Such Semitisms as occur are mostly ' secondary,' and are due to unconscious reminiscence of LXX phrases.

Luke.

His Semitisms are accountable as :

(*a*) literal translation of his Aramaic sources ;

(*b*) conscious imitation of LXX Greek. MOULTON argues that Luke would deliberately use the Biblical phraseology of the LXX when moving in Palestinian circles, for reasons of apologetic. The narrative portions of his Gospel and Acts i.–xii. show distinct affinities with Pentateuchal Greek.[2] It is suggested that Luke's style becomes more literary as he moves away from Jewish surroundings.[3]

[1] *Gram.*, vol. ii. p. 8.

[2] Cf. the characteristically Lucan καὶ ἐγένετο (see *Prolog.*, p. 16).

[3] MOULTON'S *Gram.*, vol. ii. p. 8.

1 *Peter, James, Jude.*

Slight Semitic element due to their authors thinking in Aramaic and writing in Greek, and to the influence of the LXX (especially in 1 Peter).

2 *Peter.*

Hardly any LXX influence apparent, and Semitisms are practically nil.

Matthew.

Semitisms in the first Gospel are due to Aramaic originals. The writer is himself Semitic in thought and standpoint.

Mark.

Semitisms due to Aramaic sources, and to the author's cast of mind. .

Fourth Gospel, 1–3 John.

The Greek is correct but very simple. The style shows no extensive Semitic colouring, though the priority of the verb in the sentence seems to point in that direction. But MOULTON [1] is not convinced on the latter point.

The Apocalypse.

The Semitic flavour abounds and is explained by translation from Aramaic originals and by the author's Semitic type of mind.

[1] MOULTON's *Gram.,* vol. ii. p. 32.

APPENDIX II

GRAMMATICAL AND SYNTACTICAL DEVIATIONS FROM CLASSICAL GREEK IN THE KOINH'.[1]

1. Old suffixes are dropped and new ones coined (p. 81).

2. The *nominativus pendens* construction is common (p. 90).

3. The neuter plural subject takes either a singular or plural verb.

4. The comparative serves increasingly for the superlative (cf. Matt. xi. 11).

5. The accusative gains ascendency over the dative (p. 77).

6. εἰς and ἐν are used interchangeably (p. 75).

7. The personal pronoun is more and the possessive pronoun is less frequent.

8. The optative mood is fast dropping out.

9. The use of instrumental ἐν is common (cf. Luke xxii. 49 ; 1 Cor. iv. 21).

10. Prepositions are more fluid in meaning and show a variety of uses (pp. 53, 75).

11. The rules of concord are sometimes disregarded (p. 87).

[1] The numbers in parentheses refer to examples noted in the essay.

12. The passive grows at the expense of the middle voice (cf. Matt. x. 26).

13. There is a marked increase in the use of diminutives (p. 51).

14. The dual number has disappeared.

15. Adjectives of the third declension in -ων and -υς are rare.

16. -μι verbs tend to merge into -ω verbs, and -ιζω verbs are very common (p. 83).

17. There is a distinct extension in the use of ἵνα. In classical Greek it is mostly confined to the introduction of final clauses. There are six well-defined usages of ἵνα in the N.T. (pp. 84, 90).

18. The future participle is less frequent.

19. The use of -αω and -εω verbs is confused.

20. First aorist forms like ἔσχα come into prominence.

21. The superlative adjective usually bears the elative sense (p. 86).

22. The periphrastic imperfect is common. Cf. especially Luke xv. 1 *al.*

23. General simplification showing itself in shorter sentences and constructions.

INDICES

I. SUBJECTS

II. N.T. REFERENCES

III. GREEK WORDS

187